CREATING
Vintage
Style

CREATING
Vintage
Style

**STYLISH IDEAS
& STEP-BY-STEP
PROJECTS**

LUCINDA GANDERTON

RYLAND
PETERS
& SMALL

LONDON NEW YORK

Senior Designer Megan Smith
Editor Miriam Hyslop
Picture Researcher Emily Westlake
Production Controller Gemma Moules
Art Director Anne-Marie Bulat
Editorial Director Julia Charles
Publishing Director Alison Starling

First published in the United Kingdom in 2006
by Ryland Peters & Small
20–21 Jockey's Fields
London WC1R 4BW
www.rylandpeters.com

10 9 8 7 6 5 4 3 2 1

Text © Lucinda Ganderton 2006.
Design, photographs and illustrations
© Ryland Peters & Small 2006.
The additional credits on page 112
constitute part of this copyright page.

ISBN-10: 1 84597 125 6
ISBN-13: 978 1 84597 125 0

A CIP record for this book is available
from the British Library.

Printed in China.

contents

introduction

'Contemporary vintage' is at first glance an oxymoron, but this term defines an innovative approach to interior decoration that has transformed the way we think about our homes. Although inspired by the past, it has little to do with recreating an authentic historic look with period paint colours, stencilled walls and accurate cornicing. It is not a pastiche, but is instead an eclectic, informal way of decorating, sometimes nostalgic but never cloying.

Creating vintage style involves distilling the best elements of previous decades and mixing them with the new, to create a look that is unquestionably modern and which works as well in a country hideaway as it does in an urban apartment. The inspirational interiors featured in this book show just how this can be done throughout the house, from the kitchen and dining room to your study, the children's playroom and out into the garden. All these rooms are characterized by their effortless blend of old and new furniture, fabrics, accessories and the finishing touches that make them so individual.

The pleasure in this relaxed lifestyle comes from surrounding yourself with objects that you like and enjoy, irrespective of their age or provenance, so a string of fairy lights can be hung around an engraved Venetian mirror, a set of French enamel canisters lined up under an original Habitat kitchen clock or a patchwork quilt draped happily over a new chesterfield sofa. The die-hard modernist may baulk at placing a tartan travel rug over the back of an Eileen Gray armchair, but the juxtaposition of iconic style and home comforts can be pleasing and harmonious.

There is a considerable element of imagination and originality involved in interpreting the vintage theme. Personal preferences are important, and no two people will re-work the style in the same way. It is here that an extension of the thrifty spirit of 'make do and mend', which was so necessary in less affluent eras, comes in. If you think laterally and look at your favourite possessions – whether they are family heirlooms or junk shop finds – with a fresh eye and an open mind, you will discover new and unexpected uses for them:

a lace-trimmed linen sheet can be turned into a window blind, a toast rack doubles up as a letter rack and a salvaged shop sign becomes the main decorative feature in your living room. Fine decorative antiques, glass and porcelain have always been regarded as an investment purchase, to be cared for accordingly, but there are many more affordable items to be found which are better suited to everyday use. It is better not to buy anything that is obviously in a poor state, such as a table with woodworm or tattered, threadbare curtains, but furniture and fabrics in good condition can be customised to suit your taste.

Local auction houses, car boot or jumble sales and high-street second-hand shops are the obvious starting places when setting out on the search for interesting old artefacts, but the really dedicated hunter will venture further afield, to trawl architectural salvage yards, *brocante* markets with imported furniture, fabrics and *objets d'art*, along with the regular vintage textile and interior fairs which are advertised in the specialist press. These may involve an early morning start (experienced dealers always take a torch, along with a roomy holdall)

and you are bound to find yourself sifting through piles of dismal old junk, but the reward lies in the unexpected find at the bottom of the box and in recognizing its potential.

If you are not tempted by the lure of the vintage hunt, you do have another option. There are plenty of new interpretations of old products and reproductions of classic items available, that are much easier to find and which have an authentic feel. A list of both large-scale and small, independent suppliers for many of these – including sources for familiar domestic items such as wooden scrubbing brushes, ostrich feather dusters, blue-and-white striped kitchen ceramics and galvanised watering cans – can be found at the back of the book. Most of these companies have their own shopping websites, for the Internet is now truly an international marketplace. eBay and similar sites will offer you the thrill of an auction without even having to leave home, and a few minutes surfing will locate just a few of the many dealers from across the world who offer almost anything you can imagine for sale at the press of a key.

living rooms

A contemporary living room is an informal space for unwinding and entertaining, where family and friends can listen to music, watch films or play together, surrounded by books, favourite objects, photographs and paintings. The drawing and sitting rooms of previous eras tended towards the formal and coordinated, but try not to over-design your own vintage-style living space. Take inspiration from the interior itself when planning the room scheme. Any original features – an ornate coving, folding wooden shutters or a carved marble fireplace – will set the tone for the whole décor, or you could add a new focal point such as an oversized gilt-framed mirror. Choose furniture that is easy to live with rather than grand antiques, and mix comfortable new sofas with odd armchairs. Woollen or patchwork throws and feather-filled cushions will make them even more welcoming.

ABOVE, LEFT AND RIGHT
The owners of a highly successful salvage company have put their ideas into practice at home by finding inventive new uses for sixteen crates, a school trunk and sign from a bicycle shop.

BELOW Dark floorboards, seamless cream-painted woodwork and a white sofa pull this country living space together, while recessed lighting in the window alcoves will increase the sense of space in the evening.

key elements

Colour defines both the style and mood of a room, and a harmonious palette should be the starting point when planning a living space, which is usually the busiest and most multifunctional part of the house. Natural textures and colours – either cool tones like slate and gunmetal or warmer sandstones, wood and teal – are a good, timeless choice and the palest shades are always easy to live alongside. Subtly nuanced light walls, floors and furniture create an illusion of space, and also provide a consistent background for other design elements and flashes of bright colour or pattern.

Try not to overfill your living room: even if it is comparatively large, there should be plenty of space in which to move about and to accommodate extra chairs when required. Low-level seating and tables reduce the eyelevel and will make a room seem loftier. If you are going to surround yourself with favourite vintage objects, think of it as an art gallery and position the rest of the furniture so that your treasures are set off to best advantage. Symmetrical arrangements, such as the twin sofas on either side of the fireplace above or the carefully placed looking glasses opposite, are always pleasing.

THIS PAGE The cool tones of the walls, sofa, mirrors and ottoman in this textile designer's living room are balanced with an array of bright cushions and throws that reveals her understanding of pattern and colour.

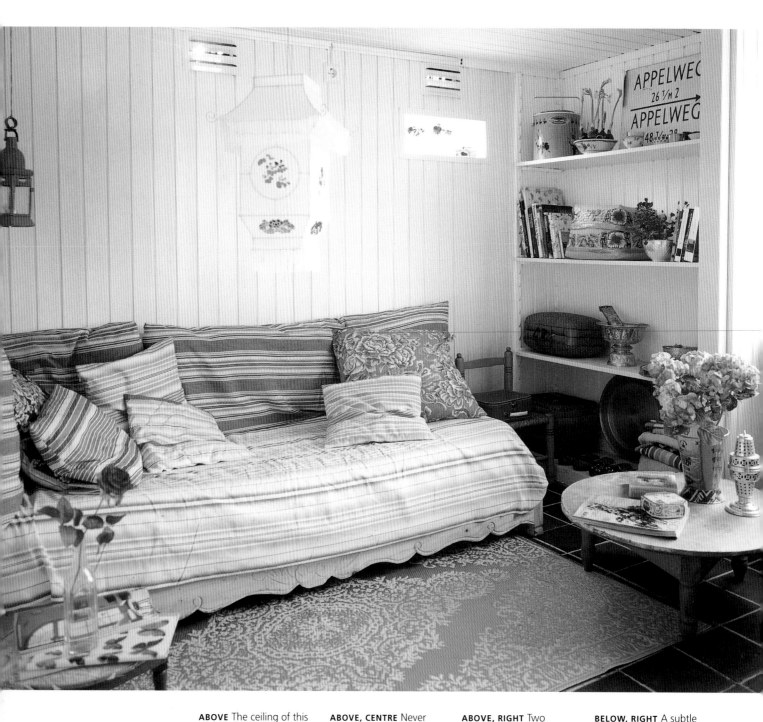

ABOVE The ceiling of this panelled room seems higher than it actually is, because the pattern and colour have been concentrated on to the divan and woven rug. The round coffee table and sparsely filled shelves increase the overall sense of space.

ABOVE, CENTRE Never be afraid to mix radically diverse styles and clashing patterns from different eras; the effect can sometimes be stunning. These two delicate oriental cushions slouch happily against a bold geometric flowered wallpaper from the 1970s.

ABOVE, RIGHT Two variations on a floral theme: as elegant today as when it was first painted in the early eighteenth century, this beautiful, classic Chinese wallpaper makes a good backdrop for a trio of idiosyncratic flowerpot handbags.

BELOW, RIGHT A subtle blend of old and new linked by a predominantly monochrome scheme: the delicate organic print of the contemporary paper complements the glass vases and funky model Eiffel tower, which seem to float against the wall on a clear Perspex table.

Although antique, the Victorian mahogany pieces known in the trade as 'brown furniture' are currently out of favour, whilst mid-twentieth-century design classics, French armoires and dressers, leather chesterfields, simple shelving and battered junkshop and flea market finds are to be found in the most relaxed and convivial rooms. These newer (and usually cheaper) pieces mix well with huge sofas and squashy armchairs to great affect.

All fashions go in cycles, and the style virtues of patterned wallpapers are currently being rediscovered. This time around, they are to be used with discretion: a single wall or a panel beside a plain chimneybreast rather than the full-on 1970s visual assault. Retro abstract designs have been reissued, as have historic prints that date back to the early eighteenth century and which would look at home in a stately mansion. Swirly carpets, on the other hand, have yet to be revived, and with good reason. White-painted or polished pine boards, sisal matting and textured carpets are far less dominating within a room scheme, and floor-level pattern now comes from rugs rather than wall-to-wall patterned Axminster.

fabrics

Vintage furnishing textiles, from folk-art patchwork quilts and cotton lace curtains to 1960s op-art roller blinds have survived in great quantities and take on a new lease of life in a contemporary living space. Some are fragile and may need to be mounted carefully as wall hangings and kept away from direct sunlight, but others, such as robust 1950s cottons, will still withstand daily use and regular washing. Older fabrics are often muted in colour and this is part of their attraction, but they were not always so subtle. Whilst William Morris earnestly persevered with traditional organic pigments in the later nineteenth century, chemists were busy producing the first synthetic dyes, in surprisingly vivid hues of purple, acid yellow, cerise and viridian. These were just as bright as the inks in a 1970s abstract print but they have faded greatly over the decades. Several manufacturers and design groups now produce copies of these washed-out floral designs, which are sought after for vintage-style homes.

FAR LEFT, BELOW
Two panels of narrow striped fabric held down with rows of brass upholstery nails are all the decoration needed on this sturdy chair.

FAR LEFT, ABOVE A row of plump, graphic cushions on a plain upholstered sofa prevent an all-white room from appearing too stark and austere.

ABOVE, LEFT These square mattress-style pads can also be used as floor cushions.

ABOVE, CENTRE Back to the decade that style forgot: 1970s prints are now highly desirable.

ABOVE, RIGHT Red, white and blue flags and cushions, adorned with simple circles of seed pearls, lend a stately air to an old armchair.

LEFT This magnificent hand-embroidered antique silk hanging, as striking as a painting, is mounted on a wooden batten so that the fabric is not put under strain.

LEFT Luscious velvet pansies add the final touch to these kitsch, flowery cushion covers.
FAR LEFT New image transfer techniques mean seaside snaps no longer need to be consigned to an album (see the project on page 22 for a similar cushion).
ABOVE, LEFT A pretty patchwork, a flowery quilt, and a pile of cushions effectively disguise an old sofa.
ABOVE, RIGHT Dress up a plain cushion with a knitted top and a few appliquéd flowers.

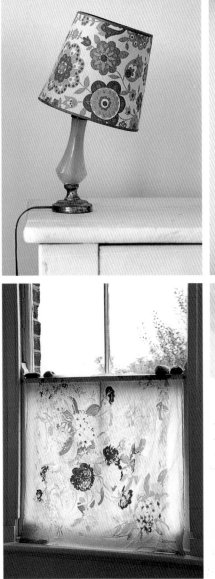

When selecting a pattern, remember that large-scale patterns should be used on bigger furniture and tinier designs – use ginghams, ditsy florals and narrow stripes on smaller pieces, so that the fabric does not engulf the furniture. Light colours or plain fabrics are a good choice for big sofas and armchairs, and will make a room appear spacious. Accents of colour and further texture can then be added with cushions and blankets.

If you prefer a less chintzy, more twentieth-century retro look, there are many later printed fabrics to be found, both originals and reproductions, and you need not limit your search to furnishing fabrics. Interiors are now more relaxed and informal than in the days of piped, frilled cushions and festoon blinds, so be innovative and think of new uses for your old bits and pieces. An interesting silk or cotton scarf can be turned into a square cushion cover with minimal sewing, draped over a lampshade (with a hole cut from the centre to prevent scorching), hung up at a window or used to tie back a curtain. Large throws or dustsheets are useful for instantly revamping sofas and chairs with less-than-perfect upholstery. Much cheaper than slipcovers, they can be layered with travel rugs or quilts for a comfortable, laid-back look.

TOP, LEFT Cover a drum lampshade with fabric by sticking it in place with double-sided tape. Trim the edges with fine braid.
TOP, RIGHT Pleated silk shades like these on a Venetian mirrored sconce can be found in charity shops or boot sales.
ABOVE, LEFT Block out the view by pinning a hemmed panel directly on to a wooden sash frame.
ABOVE, RIGHT An instant window treatment: screw a hook to the side of the frame, tie back the curtain with a scarf, then loop the knot over the hook.

MATERIALS AND EQUIPMENT

iron-on bonding web

sharp pencil

approximately 50 x 100 cm
(20 x 40 in) thin black leather

old sheet

140 cm (55 in) square of silk net

sewing kit

ethereal throw

ethereal throw A stunning combination of white net and black leather, this throw has an ethereal quality that is quite unique – the flower and leaf silhouettes seem to float across the surface of the silk. Its creator, textile artist Karen Nicol, works with leading fashion designers and her true understanding of fabrics is revealed in the pairing of such contrasting weights and textures.

1 Enlarge the flower and leaf motifs on page 102 to their full size. These shapes are all reversed and need to remain so at this stage, since you will be attaching them to the back of the leather in step 3.

2 With the paper side facing upwards, trace the outlines of the motifs on to bonding web using a sharp pencil. You will need approximately 50 motifs in total – the arrangement is quite informal so you can select the ones you like best. Cut the shapes out roughly, allowing a border of about 6 mm (¼ in) around each one.

3 Following the manufacturer's instructions carefully, iron the adhesive side of the bonding web on to the rough side of the leather, fitting the individual shapes together like a jigsaw.

4 Cut out each shape carefully, following the pencil lines. Where a motif has several elements, cut out just around the main outline at this stage.

5 Fold the old sheet in half and lay it out flat on a hard surface: a tiled or wooden floor is ideal. Put the net on top of the sheet and arrange 9–12 motifs, leather side up, in each corner of the net. Group them loosely to form a random pattern.

6 When you are satisfied with the arrangement, cut out the separate pieces of the complex motifs and space them out. Peel off the backing paper from the motifs; then, following the manufacturer's instructions, iron each shape in place using a pressing cloth to protect the surface of the leather.

transfer print cushion

Instead of keeping your old photographs tucked away, you can transfer the images on to fabric and turn them into cushions to keep for yourself, or to give as nostalgic presents. These covers feature my own favourite family black-and-white snapshots and, to complete the vintage look, I made the borders from original 1960s dressmaking material. You can print digital images directly on to transfer paper (from stationers and photographic shops) from a computer, or have your pictures copied at a high-street printer.

MATERIALS AND EQUIPMENT

old photograph

plain white cotton fabric

plain-coloured fabric (to coordinate with the patterned fabric)

matching sewing thread

patterned fabric

two matching buttons (optional)

35 x 45 cm (14 x 18 in) cushion pad

sewing kit

sewing machine

Note:

The measurements (left) are for a 15 x 25 cm (6 x 10 in) picture and a 35 x 45 cm (14 x 18 in) rectangular cushion; adapt them as necessary to fit the shape and proportions of your own photograph and pad. The seam allowance throughout is 1 cm (½ in).

CUTTING OUT

from plain-coloured fabric:

for the inner border:

two 5 x 15 cm (2 x 6 in) strips

two 5 x 30 cm (2 x 12 in) strips

for the outer border:

two 5 x 35 cm (2 x 14 in) strips

two 5 x 50 cm (2 x 20 in) strips

for the back:

one 6 x 40 cm (2½ x 16 in) strip

from patterned fabric:

for the main border:

two 10 x 20 cm (4 x 8 in) strips

two 10 x 45 cm (4 x 18 in) strips

for the back:

two 30 x 40 cm (12 x 16 in) rectangles

1 Transfer your image on to the white cotton fabric and trim it down to 15 x 25 cm (6 x 10 in).

2 With right sides facing, pin, tack and machine stitch the short plain-coloured inner border strips to the shorter sides of the picture. Carefully press the seams outwards using a pressing cloth so that the iron does not come into contact with the transferred image. Attach the two long inner borders to the long edges of the picture in the same way.

3 With right sides facing, pin, tack and machine stitch the short, then the long, patterned strips to the inner border. Press the seams inwards.

4 To complete the front panel, join on the short and long outer border strips and press the seams outwards.

5 To make the back, press under a 1 cm (½ in) turning along one long edge of the remaining coloured strip. Matching the raw edges, and with right sides together, pin, tack and machine stitch it along one long edge of a back rectangle. Press the strip outwards, then press it in half lengthways and fold it over to bind the raw edge. Pin and tack down, then stitch just inside the seam. Make two buttonholes, if you wish, 15 cm (6 in) from each side (see page 101).

6 Make a narrow double hem along one long edge of the remaining rectangle (see page 100).

7 To assemble the cover, pin the bound rectangle to the top of the front panel with right sides facing and raw edges matching. Pin the other rectangle to the bottom so that the neatened edges of the two back panels overlap.

8 Tack the three pieces together, then machine stitch around the outside edge. Clip the corners, turn right sides out and press. Insert the cushion pad and secure the opening with slip stitch (see page 101) or sew on the buttons in line with the buttonholes.

finishing touches

Once the furniture and soft furnishings have been selected, it may seem that a room scheme is fixed forever, but there are many ways in which you can change the smaller elements in order to alter the ambience and appearance of your living space. One of the most effective ways of doing this is to follow the progress of the seasons throughout the year. Most of us bring in festive decorations at Christmas time, such as the requisite ornamented tree, swags of greenery, candles and greetings cards. To reinforce this winter change and to create a cosy atmosphere you could also layer your sofa with snug throws, plaid wool blankets and extra cushions, or add a vintage chenille cloth to your table.

The warmer months, however, require a lighter touch. Spring is the time to bring the outdoors into your living space, with potted plants and vibrant fresh blooms or still-life paintings of flowers and foliage. It is easy to increase the sense of space with pale colours and unfussy fabrics: monogrammed vintage sheets can be hung at the window to diffuse the dappled sunshine or to provide instant camouflage for an old table or chair. Even something as obvious as just putting things away will change the mood.

A well-displayed collection will enhance a room, as long as it is in keeping with the overall style, but care has to be taken to prevent it looking like cluttered bric-a-brac.

OPPOSITE Metal furniture looks just as good indoors as it does in the garden, either in a conservatory or in the corner of a living room.

ABOVE, LEFT As an alternative to hanging paintings on the wall, an artist's easel can be used to display old unframed canvases, instead of the usual work in progress.

ABOVE, RIGHT Two rows of clear glass containers, each holding a single stem, have much greater visual impact than a single vase of flowers.

CENTRE, RIGHT The stalks of these roses have been cut short so that the heads mass together, forming a dome of colour like the lid of the teapot.

CENTRE, LEFT AND BELOW, LEFT Narcissus and hyacinth flowers can be forced to bloom early, providing you with a burst of unexpected colour in the late winter. Place a layer of moist bulb compost in a shallow bowl, teacup or dish. Sit the bulbs on the surface so the bottom third is covered, making sure that they do not touch each other. Keep the container in a dark, cool place, watering occasionally, until the first shoots appear, then bring them out to be enjoyed.

BELOW, RIGHT Florists store their bouquets in these galvanised buckets: brighten them up with sheets of colourful paper.

ABOVE AND RIGHT These snapshots and postcards are fixed to the wall with putty adhesive.

TOP, LEFT Perched on the end of a mantelpiece, this exquisite empty frame does not require a picture.

TOP, CENTRE Original Venetian frames are now collector's items but there are many more affordable reproductions about.

TOP, RIGHT A Victorian miniature easel shows off a precious keepsake.

If you are a magpie-like hoarder, it is worth remembering that museums only ever exhibit a small part of their holdings. By rotating and rearranging your own displays, or just putting out a few items at a time, you will show them off to best advantage. A single object on a shelf can look striking, or try grouping items together by shape or colour, so that they create their own rhythm and visual patterns. The postcard collage opposite is a good example of this approach.

It is the tiny details that really stamp an owner's personality on a room and make it unique – and this includes the fixtures and fittings, just as much as the contents. For a truly vintage look, you could go as far as replacing modern light switches with reproduction brass or Bakelite toggle switches and changing the door furniture to old china knobs or escutcheons.

kitchens & dining rooms

For generations, the kitchen has been the inevitable gathering place for every household; a place where news is exchanged and meals enjoyed by family and visitors alike. Full of activity and at the hub of domestic routine, kitchens are packed with colourful crockery, gadgets and cooking utensils. It is this functional element that lends kitchen styles from all eras a timeless appeal, which bypasses fashionable trends: a few well-chosen vintage accessories will give a comfortable, lived-in feel to even the most streamlined room. Food preparation and eating together are now part of everyday activity and most contemporary kitchens include space for a breakfast bar, if not a table and chairs. If you have the luxury of a separate dining room, this can provide the perfect setting for both formal and informal entertaining, from gourmet dinners to leisurely weekend lunches.

ABOVE Plain blue linen napkins, folded into simple triangles, lend a bright, café-like air to this chrome breakfast table and matching benches.

BELOW Wall-mounted shelves and freestanding drawers look less formal than built-in cupboards and provide plenty of display space.

key elements

All kitchens are designed around three essential features – sink, refrigerator and cooker – plus cupboards and shelves for food, pots and pans. In the past, a larder and utility room gave additional space for storage and laundry, but if you are planning a kitchen from scratch and wish to create a vintage look, many of the 'white goods' can be concealed behind cupboard doors and special units. There are, however, alternatives to a fully fitted kitchen. An Aga or range will immediately give period flavour and you can seek out retro-style fridges and washing machines in bright colours or brushed steel. Reproduction or recycled ceramic sinks (the deep ones are called 'Belfast' sinks; the shallow versions are 'Butler's') can be complemented with old-fashioned taps and a wooden draining board. Refurbish kitchen furniture from auctions or salvage yards: enamel-topped tables or butcher's blocks provide useful work surfaces. The traditional dresser with its tiered shelving was originally intended for daily use, but also as a showcase for ornamental jugs, meat dishes and the best tea set.

OPPOSITE, RIGHT This fine antique mahogany dining table was once accompanied by a set of six matching chairs. Proving that new vintage style is far from a slavish period recreation, the owner has surrounded the table with an unexpected selection of chairs: a utility seat, two Victorian Thonet bentwoods, and a woven cane chair from the mid-twentieth century.

THIS PAGE In another example of how effective mismatched seating can look, these four assorted spindle-backed kitchen chairs have been painted in toning pale pastel shades. The walls, plate rack, skirting and floorboards are all white, which gives the room a spacious, airy feeling, and the only bright colour comes from the floral ceramic dishes.

fabrics

Kitchen textiles, from ticking aprons and shelf edgings to pictorial tea towels, have an air of cosy familiarity about them. Genuinely old accessories, and those made from new fabric in vintage-style prints, can be used to soften gleaming expanses of tiled or granite surfaces and add individuality to the heart of the home. A couple of generations ago, no kitchen was complete without a handy array of peg bags, potholders, tea cosies and embroidered tray cloths. These items more or less disappeared during the minimalist late twentieth century, but they are now making a welcome comeback. They are not just nostalgic, but also practical: clean, old linen drying cloths, for example, can be put to daily use and are still the best way to polish fine glassware.

Antique table linen, both plain and embroidered, is plentiful and easy to source: even if you cannot find a complete set, a damask cloth and eight non-matching white napkins can look striking, particularly if they all have different edgings or initials. The fabric can be revived by washing at a high temperature and pressing with a hot iron whilst slightly damp. Spray-on starch or silicon stiffener will restore a clean, crisp finish. Elsewhere in the kitchen, vintage curtains can be laundered, ironed and altered to fit your own windows, to keep draughts away from the back door, or fitted on sprung wire under draining boards and work surfaces.

OPPOSITE, ABOVE RIGHT Checked fabrics always look bright and cheerful.

OPPOSITE, BELOW Hide your modern appliances behind a 1950s curtain.

ABOVE To make a runner, cut a long rectangle, half the width of the table, and allow a 10 cm (4 in) overhang at each end. Hem all round and trim with toning tassels, braid and a pleated frill.

ABOVE, CENTRE Store matching napkins in sets by tying them together with braid or ribbon.

ABOVE, RIGHT This handle cover is made from two pieces of felted wool.

RIGHT Oilcloth and plastic-coated tablecloths are practical, yet stylish.

BELOW, RIGHT Cutlery rolls are ideal for picnics.

BELOW, CENTRE Make this holder by pressing the corners of a napkin to the centre. Sew three sides together and sew a fastener to the fourth.

BELOW, LEFT These monogrammed napkins were once an essential part of a girl's trousseau.

apron Even a novice cook will be transformed into an accomplished domestic goddess by this retro-style reversible apron. Designer Emily Medley has used two bold geometric prints, in a characteristic 1970s yellow, orange and brown colour scheme, and both sides have a large and practical pocket. Only basic sewing skills are needed to put it all together and the effect is stunning.

MATERIALS AND EQUIPMENT

main cotton fabric

contrast cotton fabric

matching sewing thread

sewing machine

sewing kit

CUTTING OUT
apron

For the front, cut a 85 x 100 cm (33 x 40 in) rectangle from the main fabric. Fold in half, long edges together, with right sides facing. Pin together along the top and half of the side edges. Mark a point on the top 28 cm (11 in) in from the corners and a second point on the sides 30 cm (12 in) down. Draw a curve to join the points. Pin just inside the line, then cut along it. Cut the back to the same size from the contrast fabric.

from the contrast print cut:

tabs: two 4 x 15 cm (1½ x 6 in) strips
ties: two 6 x 92 cm (2½ x 36 in) strips
neck loop: 6 x 60 cm (2½ x 24 in) strip
appliqué: Cut out two life-sized wooden-spoon shapes from the contrast print.

pockets

From the main fabric, cut a 25 x 50 cm (10 x 20 in) rectangle. Fold in half, short edges together, and draw a curve across one corner. Pin both layers together just inside the curve, then cut out. Cut another pocket from the contrast fabric to the same shape.

1 Pin and tack the two 'spoons' to the front of the apron, one on each side, 20 cm (8 in) from the top. Set the machine to a zigzag stitch and sew around the edges.

2 Fold under and press a 2 cm (⅝ in) double hem along the top of each pocket. Machine stitch close to the inner fold. Cut small notches along the curves, then press under 2 cm (⅝ in) around the raw edges.

3 To make the tabs, press each strip in half, long sides together, with wrong sides facing, then press a 1 cm (½ in) turning along each long edge and refold. Pin and tack the edges together, then work a row of machine stitch 3 mm (⅛ in) in from each side.

4 Fold one tab into a loop and tack to the wrong side of the pocket, 15 cm (6 in) from the right corner. Do the same with the second tab on the other pocket.

5 Pin and tack the first pocket to the front, covering the ends of the spoons, and machine stitch close to the edge. Work a second line of stitches 1 cm (½ in) further in. Sew the second pocket to the back in the same way.

6 Make up the neck loop and ties as for the tabs, pressing under one short end of each tie to neaten. Pin and tack the neck loop to the right side of the front, 1 cm (½ in) in from the top corners, raw edges together. Pin and tack the open ends of the ties in place on the side edges, 1 cm (½ in) down from the bottom of the curve, raw edges together.

7 With right sides facing and the neck loop and ties drawn into the middle, pin and tack the front and back together, leaving the bottom edge open. Clip the corners, then turn right side out and press. Press under a 2 cm (¾ in) hem around the open edge, then pin, tack and machine stitch the edge together.

finishing touches

ABOVE, LEFT These quirky egg cosies are made from quarter-circles cut from densely felted wool and stitched into cones.

ABOVE, CENTRE White table linen and classic cutlery are a timeless combination; add an elegant touch by tying a ribbon bow around a silver cake knife.

ABOVE, RIGHT Look out for old pint milk bottles, especially those printed with advertising slogans or the name of a dairy.

RIGHT No afternoon tea tray is complete without a crochet jug cover; make your own by sewing glass beads around the border of a dainty lace mat.

LEFT A fluted cup from grandmother's best tea set makes the perfect container for a single old-fashioned bloom, like this subtle-hued anemone.

OPPOSITE A varied assortment of 1970s tins shares a characteristically vivid colour scheme.

Along with treasured pottery, glassware and canteens of cutlery, many old kitchen utensils still survive after decades of continued use. Balance scales with brass weights, hand-turned coffee grinders and loaf tins can be found at antique markets or specialist dealers, and there is great pleasure to be had in putting them to their original purpose (if they are clean and still in good condition). They can otherwise simply be collected as decorative objects and grouped by colour, type or pattern.

Old white ceramic jelly moulds, storage containers with stencilled lettering and pressed glass cake stands are far more ornamental than their modern counter-parts, but if you cannot locate the originals there are some kitchen classics that are still in production. English pottery firm T. G. Green and Company has manufactured its signature blue-and-white striped Cornish Ware in the Midlands since the 1920s, and nearby at Church Gresley, Mason Cash still create traditional embossed mixing bowls from the local clay. Other items remain unchanged: a new wooden spoon, lemon squeezer or balloon whisk is more or less indistinguishable from one that was made 50 years ago. Some, more ephemeral, objects were not intended to last for a long time and survive only by default.

ABOVE LEFT Old enamel strainers, in a range of subtly muted colours, make an effective display. ABOVE RIGHT This carefully selected assortment of nineteenth-century French enamel kitchenware is both decorative and practical. BELOW A row of vintage postcards enlivens the dreary task of washing up: protect them with a piece of glass or Perspex.

Stoneware jars, commemorative tins and canisters, or moulded glass bottles, are now much sought after. They look very effective displayed alongside new, inexpensive collectibles: colourful food packaging from Thai or Chinese supermarkets, interesting sardine or drinks tins or flower-painted Thermos flasks.

When it comes to kitchen china, the days of the vast dinner service, complete with three sizes of plates, several tureens and oval serving dishes, are long gone: few of us have the space to store so much crockery and entertaining is far less formal. You can, however, make a special mealtime seem unique with a few well-chosen details. Napkin rings, a small posy of flowers or a bow on the stem of a glass will all make a place setting seem special. Matching tea sets were also once commonplace but you can create a new twist on the theme by hanging your odd cups on hooks under shelves or units. Afternoon tea itself is a relaxing social event that is ripe for revival: a tray arranged with a dainty embroidered cloth, a jug of milk, a china teapot and a bowl of sugar lumps – whether coordinated or not – has its own particular charm.

LEFT Prettily decorated cups and saucers are evocative of more sedate days: collect a mismatched set and invite your friends round for tea and cakes.
BELOW, RIGHT Tie a spray of lily of the valley with organza ribbon and lay it across a wine glass as an individual favour.
BELOW, CENTRE A pink hydrangea head has been fixed to the back of this chair with a loosely tied ribbon bow – a personal touch for a special party.
BELOW, LEFT Sometimes the smallest details can be the most effective: the fluted border of the dinner plate echoes the simple bead trim on these brown linen napkins.

heart of fresh roses

Set the scene for a special lunch or dinner party with this romantic garland, designed by Paula Pryke. A heart-shaped foam base makes the perfect framework for a delicate display of fragrant pink 'Anna' roses, palest green guelder rose and lacy white hydrangeas, which can be used as a table centrepiece or hung from the dining-room wall.

MATERIALS AND EQUIPMENT

heart-shaped floral foam base,
43 cm (17 in) across at widest point

50 cm (20 in) green velvet ribbon,
3.5 cm (1½ in) wide (optional)

30 pink roses (*Rosa* 'Anna')

27 sprigs guelder rose
(*Viburnum opulus*)

6 white hydrangeas
(*Hydrangea macrophylla*)

florist's knife

heavy-gauge stub wire

florist's scissors

1 Soak the heart-shaped foam base in water for five minutes. Then, using a florist's knife, trim away a strip of foam about 2.5 cm (1 in) wide on both the inner and outer edges. This will make the base more three-dimensional.

2 If you plan to hang the garland, tie the velvet ribbon around the top of the foam base with a double knot. To prevent it from slipping, bend a stub wire into a U-shape and push it into the foam so that it straddles the ribbon and pins it in place.

3 Using florist's scissors, trim the stems of the roses to within 5 cm (2 in) of the rose heads. Arrange the roses around the heart shape, inserting the stems so that the flowers face to the right and left of the base.

4 When you have laid the foundation of pink roses, fill in the heart with guelder rose. Cut down the stems to 5 cm (2 in) and insert the green florets of guelder rose around the roses on the inner and outer edges.

5 Divide each hydrangea flower into two or three groups of florets. Finish off the display by filling in any remaining exposed areas of foam on the heart shape with small groups of these delicate white flowers.

bedrooms

Whether you long for a flower-strewn boudoir, fantasise about the fifties chic of a glamour puss, or simply yearn for a comfortable retreat at the end of the day, your bedroom is the one place where you can truly express your individual style within your own personal space. We spend up to a third of our day in our bedrooms and, although much of that time is passed sleeping, it is important to create a tranquil ambience for cosseting, romance and rest alike. A vintage-themed décor, with its seamless combination of old and new, will give you the best of all worlds, whatever the age and style of your home. Succumb to your inner nesting instinct and surround yourself with the home comforts of a previous era: patchwork quilts, paisley eiderdowns, bolsters and old-fashioned counterpanes, but don't stint when it comes to hunting down suitable new downy feather pillows and a bouncy, well-sprung mattress to accompany them.

key elements

A serene atmosphere is conducive to peaceful sleep, so aim to create a calm mood in your bedroom. Too much colour and pattern can prove overwhelming, but by starting out with a neutral background of pale walls, floors and ceiling, you can add an assortment of curtains, rugs and accessories without the overall look becoming too cluttered. Remember that built-in cupboards take up less space than wardrobes, and look out for old vanity, cheval or wall mirrors, which will add an airy feeling by reflecting light back into the room.

The bed is, inevitably, the most dominant feature, but careful choice of linen and covers will reduce the visual impact. Old wooden and metal bedsteads are characterful, but were not designed for modern comfort. Check the springing or base slats before buying and make sure you get a supportive new mattress. There are also many reproduction beds on the market, which are wider than the originals. New paint will soften the look of dark-coloured wooden bedsteads and other old furniture and turn junk-shop finds into one-off pieces. Strip the wax or existing paint from old pine washstands, wardrobes and dressing tables, and repaint with one of the many shades of off-white paint.

ABOVE, LEFT Original or period French armoires are perfect for storing clothes. To keep out dust and moths, remove any wire panels and replace them with safety glass. Staple a length of fabric – either plain or with a bold pattern – inside the frame to conceal the contents. The floral chintz used here complements perfectly the monochrome Toile de Jouy cherub print on the adjacent full-length curtains perfectly.

BELOW, LEFT Once the place where a 1920s flapper completed her toilette, this wooden dressing table with its long oval mirror and useful drawers has been given a fresher, more contemporary look with a coat of off-white paint in a satin finish. An embroidered pashmina, chosen to harmonise with the lush flowered curtains, has been thrown over the padded stool as a more relaxed alternative to an upholstered seat.

LEFT In an undeniably contemporary setting an old quilted bedspread effectively softens the industrial lines of a steel bed frame.

MAIN PICTURE Expanses of plain white paintwork give this bedroom a light and airy feel, and provide an understated backdrop for the eclectic accessories.

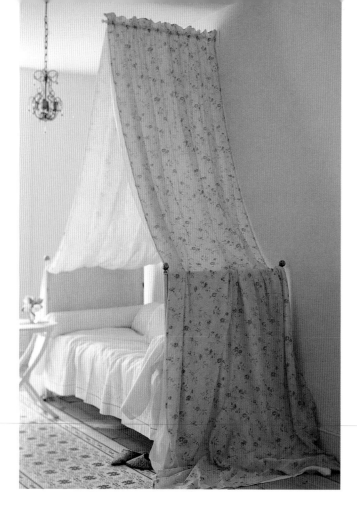

voile bed canopy The elegant cascades of this Regency-style flowery drape, from leading soft furnishings expert Katrin Cargill, lend an air of romance to a classic bedroom. Although the effect is dramatic, it is surprisingly easy to put together from a length of floaty voile gathered on to a short curtain pole, then attached to the wall with a bracket.

MATERIALS AND EQUIPMENT

floral voile

plain cotton for lining

short wooden curtain pole
with bracket and finial

sewing machine

sewing kit

1 Centre the bracket above the bed and fix it securely to the wall with long screws. Measure the distance from the top of the bracket to the floor. Add 1 m (1 yd) to this measurement, plus 20 cm (8 in) for the hem. Double this figure for your final length of fabric: a single furnishing width will be sufficient.

2 Cut the voile in half across the width. With right sides facing and the pattern running in the same direction on each panel, pin and tack the two top edges together with a 2 cm (⅔ in) seam. Press open.

3 Cut a length of cotton lining to the same length as the uncut voile. Fold it in half across the width and press the fold.

4 Press under a double 1 cm (½ in) hem (see page 100) along the long edges of the voile, then press under a double 4 cm (1½ in) turning along the short edges. Mitre the corners (see page 101), then pin, tack and machine stitch the hem around all four edges.

5 Neaten the lining fabric in the same way, but turn up a double 8 cm (3 in) hem along the short edges to make it slightly shorter than the voile.

6 Place the voile on a flat surface with the right side down. Lay the lining on top, right side up; the wrong sides are now together. Align the centre seam on the voile with the pressed fold in the lining. Pin and tack the two pieces of fabric together along this line.

7 Fold the canopy along the seam so that the lining is on the inside. Tack through all four layers about 2 cm (¾ in) below the fold to prevent it from slipping.

8 Using a dressmaker's pen, mark two parallel lines for the casing across the width of the canopy. The first should be 5 cm (2 in) below the fold and the second a further 3 cm (1¼ in) beneath that. Pin and tack along the lines and check that the pole fits into the casing. Adjust the position of the second line if necessary, then machine stitch along both lines.

9 Insert the pole into the casing and adjust the ruffles evenly. Slot the finial on to the pole, and then screw the other end into the bracket.

fabrics

FAR LEFT This well-worn but much-loved Victorian patchwork is made entirely from silk diamonds embellished with hand embroidery.
LEFT To make a scented lavender or rose sachet, sew two rectangles of fabric together around three sides, turn right side out and fill with a handful of dried flowers. Slip stitch the fourth edge closed, then bind with ribbon.
BOTTOM AND BELOW, LEFT AND RIGHT Use bows of satin or organza ribbon to add a feminine touch to blankets, curtains and cushions.

RIGHT Turn an unused alcove into storage space by hanging floral curtains from a rail fixed at ceiling height. Keep them drawn back to showcase a pretty summer frock within.
FAR RIGHT Sew scraps of old lace and cutwork mats on to small cushions, then fill with pot pourri so they release their fragrance when moved.
RIGHT, BELOW This stack of assorted vintage eiderdowns shows how different patterns will merge together when they share a common colour scheme.

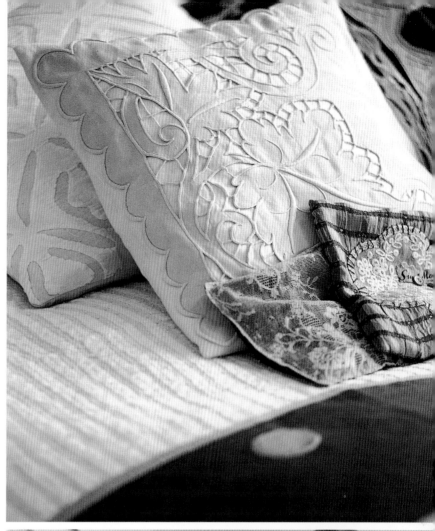

As the bedroom's largest piece of furniture and main focal point, your bed provides the ideal background for showing off an assortment of interesting textile pieces. Layered accessories always give a more stylish look than a single large cover, so display neatly folded antique quilts, brightly coloured crochet afghans or a pile of flowery cushions against basic white sheets and pillowcases. This is a quick way to transform the look of your bedroom, and one which you can easily change to match the seasons – cuddle up to fluffy woollen blankets and satin eiderdowns during the winter and keep cool in the warmer months with Egyptian cotton sheets and a mosquito net or draped voile canopy. If you have an attractive old-style wrought-iron or brass bedstead, make the most of it by hanging simple fabric bags for nighttime necessities from the frame. On the other hand, a bulky divan base can be played down with a fitted white cotton valance and a sheet or cotton throw draped over a padded headboard.

Antique bedlinen, especially that from France and Eastern Europe, has become highly sought after in recent years and specialist dealers now import these fabrics in bulk. Old hemp or pure linen sheets and pillowcases have an unmistakable feel that only comes from decades of washing and

TOP, LEFT These three coordinating drawstring linen bags – ideal for lingerie – hang neatly from loops at the back. **TOP, RIGHT** Covered coat hangers protect your garments and look pretty in the wardrobe. **ABOVE, RIGHT** Vintage fabrics and part of an old quilt are combined with checked linen and ticking stripes to make a patchwork bag. **ABOVE, LEFT** New bedlinen with a versatile spotty print works well alongside a faded vintage floral bolster.

ironing, and often feature beautifully embroidered monograms dating from their days as part of a young bride's trousseau. Look out also for turn-backs featuring hand-stitched mottoes or lace edgings, along with delicate openwork or hemstitching trims – or add your own to plain linen. Undersized or damaged sheets can be cut down and reused as cushion or pillow covers or incorporated into patchwork designs. Remember that even the smallest scraps and remnants can be used to cover padded coat hangers or pieced together to make drawstring bags in which to store everything from the laundry to cosmetics.

Although eiderdowns and blankets have long been superseded by the more practical duvets, they are always useful for adding extra warmth and colour. Old fringed Welsh rugs, with their muted chequerboard patterns, will sit happily alongside new mohair or plaids. Plain bed blankets are traditionally finished with satin ribbon: stitch a border of narrow ribbon into open-weave wool as a twist on this theme. Elsewhere, cotton tape, braid and silky ribbons can be tied into bows to make cushion cover closures, curtain tabs or simply to lend a pretty and slightly frivolous air to an ultra-feminine bedroom.

THIS PICTURE Translucent lacy fabric in pale colours always looks glamorous: these girly bags are trimmed with shiny ribbon bows and antique buckles.

ABOVE Not all your clothes have to be put away: too pretty to hide, this vintage blouse is the perfect complement to the rose-print paper on the wall behind.
RIGHT A collection of interesting patterned handkerchiefs from the mid-twentieth century is displayed on a miniature ladder.
FAR RIGHT Cover your old hot water bottles with knitted woollen fabric recycled from an outworn cardigan, then snuggle up cosily on a chilly winter night.

MATERIALS AND EQUIPMENT

a selection of old and new fabrics
of similar weight

rotary cutter (optional)

quilter's ruler (optional)

cutting mat (optional)

30 cm (12 in) square of thick paper
to use as a template

175 cm (69 in) square of
backing fabric

four 10 x 175 cm (4 x 69 in) wide
strips of plain fabric for the border

matching sewing thread

sewing machine

sewing kit

diamond patchwork bedcover The charm of this traditional

patchwork lies in the apparent randomness of the fabrics and the interesting variety of colours used by designer Jeanie Blake. One diagonally striped square block is repeated to create a pattern of concentric diamonds. To achieve a similar spontaneous look, try not to be over-careful or contrived when selecting and arranging your materials.

1 Sort out and press your fabrics, which should all be cotton and of a similar weight. Cut them into narrow strips of between 5 cm (2 in) and 10 cm (4 in) wide. A rotary cutter and quilter's ruler, which enable you to cut quickly and accurately, will speed up this process, but are not essential.

2 Choose a 15 cm (6 in) strip for the centre. Cut a length of different fabric, and trim the ends at 45 degrees. Pin and tack together, then machine stitch with a 6 mm (¼ in) seam (see page 100). Press the seam outwards. Do the same on the other side, and then add further strips, each shorter than the last, until you have a square. Check the size against the template as you work.

3 Place the template on top of the completed block and draw around it with a dressmaker's pen. Cut out around the line. Make another 35 blocks in the same way, each one different.

4 Lay the blocks out in six rows of six, alternating the direction of the fabric to form an overall diamond design. Take some time arranging them so that you get the best balance of pattern and colour within the design.

5 With right sides facing, pin, tack and machine stitch the first two pairs of blocks together with a 1 cm (½ in) seam. Press the seams to opposite sides, then join the two pairs to make a large square. Sew the remaining blocks together to make eight more squares, and then join the squares into three rows. Complete by seaming the rows together.

6 Lay the backing fabric on the floor with the right side facing downwards. Place the patchwork centrally on top with the right side upwards and pin together around the outside edge, smoothing the layers from the centre to ensure they lie flat. Tack together 1 cm (½ in) from the edge, then trim away the surplus backing fabric.

7 Press under 1 cm (½ in) along each side of the four strips of plain fabric, then press each one in half lengthways. Fold the first strip over one edge of the quilt and pin, then tack in place. Stitch down by hand or machine and trim the binding in line with the corners.

8 Pin a folded strip to the next edge and trim 1 cm (½ in) from the end adjacent to the first strip. Press the overlap to the wrong side. Tack, then stitch the strip down, and finish off the folded corner with slip stitch (see page 101). Repeat for the other two edges.

finishing touches

ABOVE, LEFT A Florence Nightingale-style concertina night light holder is suspended from the foot of a bedstead.

ABOVE, CENTRE The filigree wirework of this tulip-shaped candleholder will cast a delicate lattice of shadows across the windowsill.

ABOVE, RIGHT The flower and leaf-shaped shadows from this old French metal sconce dance and flicker across the wall behind.

RIGHT Billowing, sheer curtains filter the light as it enters your bedroom by day and provide privacy at night. Tie them back with a broad gauzy bow: the black ribbon used here is a pleasing accent that echoes the baroque curves of the furniture.

LEFT A simple shade of softly gathered organza makes a delicate shade for a clear glass lamp.

RIGHT Disparate objects will always harmonise if they have a common theme: hang them on a peg rail against an off-white wall to create the maximum effect. **CENTRE, RIGHT** Pin a collection of insect and flower brooches to a board instead of keeping them in a jewellery box. **CENTRE, LEFT** For this informal dressing table, display jewels are simply hung from the neck of translucent glass vases. **BOTTOM, LEFT** Enjoy your necklaces all the time by pinning them up. **BOTTOM, RIGHT** Victorian ladies displayed their brooches on small padded cushions like this.

It is always pleasing to surround yourself with beautiful objects, and the bedroom is the perfect intimate place to put out all those small collections that would look lost in larger or busier spaces elsewhere in the house. In addition to the china pin dolls, pressed-glass ring stands, perfume atomisers and swansdown powder puffs that adorned our grandmothers' dressing tables, you are bound to have acquired a host of attractive items that could be displayed. Turn out your cupboards and jewellery boxes in search of handbags, accessories and strings of pearls or glass beads that you would appreciate looking at every day. Group your treasures according to theme, colour or shape and set them out on delicate console tables, sets of shelves or even a simple pinboard so that they look like small still-life arrangements.

Set the atmosphere with soft, low level lighting: adjustable dimmer switches can be easily fitted to bright overhead lights and bedside lamps to provide a gentle glow. Old fitments are often more interesting than their modern counterparts, but you must ensure that they are checked over by a qualified electrician. Cotton-covered flex looks more authentic than plastic cable and can be bought from specialist lighting shops. Candlelight is flattering and romantic: there are a host of period-style nightlights, lanterns and wall sconces around, which come with the inevitable safety warning – 'Never leave a lighted candle unattended'!

diamanté cushion

Textile designer Karen Nicol is an inveterate collector with the true expert's eye for the quirky and the unusual. Her studio is a real treasure trove, the accumulation of long hours spent scouring markets and car boot sales for vintage costume jewellery, silk flowers, buttons, beads and ribbons, all of which influence or are incorporated into her work. This sparkling cushion is a wonderful showcase for a collection of diamanté buckles, brooches and dress clips.

1 Clean all the pieces of jewellery with a soft cloth and check that all the paste jewels are fixed. Use a pair of small pliers to secure the settings as necessary.

MATERIALS AND EQUIPMENT

two 50 cm (20 in) squares of fine soft suede or suede-look fabric

matching sewing thread

45 cm (18 in) square cushion pad

19 brooches and buckles

low-tack masking tape

small pliers

sewing kit

2 Choose one of the larger items to be the centre of the arrangement and place this in the middle of one suede square. Lay seven small buckles in a circle around it.

3 Arrange the remaining pieces around the edge in a circle, leaving a margin of at least 5 cm (2 in) around the outside. The final look will depend very much on the size and shape of your own jewellery.

4 When you are happy with the arrangement, use a dressmaker's pen to mark the position of each piece with a couple of tiny dots. Put them all down on the back panel in roughly the same layout, so that you will remember where each one goes.

5 Pin the brooches in place. Sew the clips and buckles down with a few stitches, using a double length of a sewing thread the same colour as the suede.

6 With right sides facing outwards, fix the front and back together around three sides. Use tiny strips of low-tack masking tape, spaced approximately 8 cm (3 in) apart. Insert the pad inside the cover and tape the remaining side.

7 Carefully machine stitch the front and back together 2 cm (¾ in) from the edge, peeling each piece of tape just before it goes under the presser foot.

bathrooms

Decades of modernisation and makeovers mean that older homes rarely retain their original sanitary fittings, but a few well-chosen period-style accessories will give a more relaxed ambience to the most spartan surroundings, and transform a clinical bathroom into a personal sanctuary for pampering and indulgence. Victorian houses and apartments often have bright, high-ceilinged bathrooms with sash windows and space for freestanding furniture, which were converted from a spare bedroom or dressing room. More modern, purpose-built bathrooms tend to be smaller and boxier, with fully fitted bath, sink and WC. Whatever the size, a classic white suite is the best starting point and, as with any other room, it is the choice of details that will create the overall atmosphere – whether you prefer an invigorating morning shower or a scented, candle-lit soak in essential oils at the end of the day.

ABOVE, LEFT Optimise your storage by using all the 'hidden space' you can find, in an imaginative way. An old glass vitrine cabinet – of the type more usually found in a living room – has been painted with blue gloss and fixed into the shallow recess behind the head of the fitted panelled bath in this individual bathroom.

ABOVE, RIGHT A striking feature piece like this antique French enamel sink and splashback will always take centre stage: maintain the impact by keeping to a plain colour for the walls and flooring.

BELOW More atypical bathroom furniture: the combination of old wood and a new roll-top bath is cool and sophisticated.

key elements

Just as the bed is the dominant feature in any bedroom, the bath always sets the style for the bathroom. If your own tub is less than perfect, play it down by emphasising other aspects within the scheme, but if you are starting from scratch you will have a wide range of baths and sinks from which to choose. Modernist DIY manuals from the mid-twentieth century exhorted householders to board in or replace resplendent Victorian cast-iron baths, but these are now highly desirable. The originals can be found in reclamation yards but may prove just too big and heavy for contemporary rooms (and impossible to get up the stairs). There are, fortunately, plenty of reproduction suites, some made on a smaller scale and all manufactured from lighter materials.

Freestanding furniture adds style to a larger bathroom, but if you do not have the space for a washstand, laundry box or set of drawers, you can create additional storage by installing a cupboard around the washbasin, or hanging towels from a wall- or ceiling-mounted rack. To end on a practical note, remember that all bathroom surfaces should be water-resistant to guard against splashes, dampness and condensation. Varnish wooden furniture, seal floorboards and use special 'kitchen and bathroom' paints, which contain anti-fungicide for the walls.

THIS PICTURE Two model
yachts perched on an
airing rack and a few blue
stripes are all it needs to
create a nautical look.
INSET A lifebelt, blue
walls and a tiny flotilla,
overseen by Pinocchio,
give an upbeat, more
obviously seaside air
to a family bathroom.

RIGHT Drawstring bags come in a range of sizes to contain anything from cosmetics to laundry. Save space by hanging them from handles or a peg rail.

MAIN PICTURE A full-length flowered curtain, made from easily washed unlined cotton, is the only element of pattern in this understated bathroom.

fabrics

Towels, shower curtains and bathmats all have a functional role to play in the bathroom, but they do not have to be strictly utilitarian. Textiles are a good way to introduce colour and pattern to a neutrally decorated bathroom, and they will also soften the effect of tiles, glass and chrome. Vintage fabrics, in particular, can be used to emphasise existing period features, or to add character to a more modern bathroom.

Chintzy curtains always work well at windows, but they can also be used to cover the bath. Hem a panel to a same-sized waterproof shower curtain, insert eyelets along the top edge in corresponding positions, then fix the curtain rings through both curtains and hang in place.

Try mixing florals with the representational prints that were fashionable in the 1950s. These have a kitsch charm that is hard to resist: look out for ladylike patterns featuring lipsticks, perfume bottles or powder compacts. Small remnants can be added to plain towels or made into simple drawstring bags. Old hand towels and individual guest towels made from waffle-weave fabric or huckaback are often embroidered with flowers or initials and finished off with crochet lace. These look attractive when folded and hung from a clothes horse or wooden towel rail, even if they are not used daily.

ABOVE, LEFT A wide band of vintage 1950s furnishing fabric and a striped ribbon trim this plain hand towel.

ABOVE, RIGHT This pretty sheer curtain, perfect for screening a bathroom window, was made by stitching together a unique collection of vintage flower-printed handkerchiefs.

BELOW, RIGHT An eclectic assembly of textile prints adds colour to the plain tiles of a 1930s bathroom.

BELOW, LEFT Edge a towel with a border of woven braid and white lace.

floral dorothy bag

Designer Caroline Zoob works from a studio in the English countryside, where she creates textile pieces with a fine attention to detail which all combine modern sensibility with a period style. She has an affinity with antique materials and made this drawstring bag – which is just right for holding your favourite cosmetics and toiletries – from a 1930s fabric remnant.

MATERIALS AND EQUIPMENT

antique fabric for the bag

white linen for the lining

41 cm (16 in) length of piping cord

two 50 cm (20 in) lengths of blind cord

matching sewing thread

sewing machine

sewing kit

small safety pin

CUTTING OUT

bag (antique fabric)

for the sides: two 20 x 22 cm (8 x 9 in) rectangles

for the base: one 14 cm (5½ in) diameter circle

3 x 41 cm (1¼ in x 16 in) border strip

3 x 41 cm (1¼ in x 16 in) bias strip cut with diagonal ends both sloping in the same direction for the piping

lining (white linen)

two 20 x 22 cm (8 x 9 in) rectangles

one 14 cm (5½ in) diameter circle

1 Mark the position of the drawstring channel with two points on each long side of each bag rectangle, 4.5 and 5.5 cm (1¾ and 2¼ in) down from the top corners. With right sides facing, pin and tack together and join the long sides with a 1 cm (½ in) seam, leaving the space between the marks unstitched. Press the seam open.

2 Join the short ends of the border strip, right sides facing, with a 1 cm (½ in) seam. Press the seam open. With wrong sides facing, fold and press the border in half along the long edge. Turn the bag right side out, then pin and tack the border around the top, matching the raw edges and the seam.

3 With right sides facing, sew the diagonal ends of the bias strip together to form a loop, then press the seam open.

4 Join the ends of the piping cord with slip stitch, overlapping them by 1 cm (½ in). With wrong sides facing, fold the fabric loop in half over the cord and tack in place close to the cord.

5 Matching the raw edges and seam, pin and tack the round of piping to the bottom of the bag. Cut a series of 6 mm (¼ in) notches, approximately 2.5 cm (1 in) apart, through all three layers of seam allowance.

6 Turn the bag wrong side out. With right sides facing, pin and tack the base to the bottom of the bag and machine stitch 1 cm (½ in) from the edge using a zip foot.

7 Pin and tack the two pieces of lining together, then machine stitch along the long sides 12 mm (½ in) from the edge. Leave a 5cm (2 in) gap at the bottom of one seam for turning the bag right side out. Notch and join the base as in steps 5 and 6.

8 With right sides facing, fit the lining inside the bag, matching the side seams. Pin and tack together around the top, then machine stitch, leaving a seam allowance of just over 1 cm (½ in exactly).

9 Turn the bag right side out through the gap in the lining, then close the gap with slip stitch. Push the lining back inside the bag and press lightly.

10 Rule two parallel lines with a dressmaker's pen to join the top and bottom of the gaps in the side seams on both front and back. Tack the two layers together between them. Work two rounds of machine stitch along the lines around the bag to form the drawstring channel.

11 Fix a small safety pin to one end of a length of cord and thread it through one side of the channel, and out of the opposite opening. Knot the ends together and trim. Thread the other cord through the channel on the other side, then knot the ends and trim.

12 Cut a pentagon shape, approximately 5 cm (2 in) deep, from the remaining antique fabric, and press under a 6 mm (¼ in) hem all round. Fold in half over one of the knots, then tack in place. Slip stitch around the edges. Finish off the other cord in the same way.

finishing touches

CENTRE, LEFT Cluster small groups of attractive old and new perfume bottles on shelves or beside the washbasin.

CENTRE, RIGHT This fine transfer-printed antique sink retains its original brass cross-head brass taps, which come complete with ceramic labels to distinguish 'hot' from 'cold': similar reproductions would give style to a modern basin.

BELOW, RIGHT When hanging items from a tiled wall, always fix the nail or screw into the grout so you can change the position or remove it.

BELOW, LEFT A hand towel with a woven, lettered border and a shell-shaped enamel soap dish will make a guest feel welcome and cared for.

TOP, LEFT Keep a spoon at hand to measure fragrant bath salts into steaming water.

TOP, RIGHT Shades of white on white always look chic and add a sense of space to the smallest bathroom.

OPPOSITE, ABOVE This striking patchwork splashback is made from a collection of blue and white Victorian tiles assembled over time.

OPPOSITE, BELOW RIGHT Antique cologne, smelling salt and perfume bottles often have silver stoppers and collars: check the hallmark stamps to find out their exact age.

OPPOSITE, BELOW LEFT An array of luscious, rose-printed Edwardian postcards gives a facelift to a plain cream wall.

Bathroom accessories are not just limited to functional soap holders, towel rails and medicine cabinets. All bathrooms have a looking glass over the sink – it is essential for washing, shaving and hairstyling – but further mirrors can be positioned elsewhere to reflect sunshine back into a room, increasing the sense of space. Ornate picture frames make decorative alternatives to a plain mirror surround.

You can exhibit one-off vintage finds such as old shaving brushes and soap dishes to great advantage against mirrors, shiny tiles or along narrow shelves. Try decanting toiletries, essential oils or bath salts into cut glass or coloured bottles and jars, and arrange them along a windowsill where they will catch the light, or show off exquisitely wrapped soaps in open baskets or small cupboards with wide open doors. Some packaging, especially that with retro-style labelling, is just too pretty to discard once empty: this too can be collected and displayed.

children's rooms

With great speed, a child's bedroom has to evolve from a simple nursery for sleeping into a private world of make-believe, then a den for playing with friends and, in time, a place for study and homework. With imagination, flexibility, and maybe a little nostalgia for your own childhood, you can meet these changing requirements, but take your child's own whims into account along the way. You may find yourself compromising with Thomas the Tank Engine curtains, or superhero duvet cases as young interior designers make their own contribution, but these tastes tend to pass quickly. The charms of pull-along wooden toys, wind-up trains and irresistible teddy bears appeal to all ages, and shabby chic rose prints may, in the end, prove just as pleasing as Barbie-pink flounces.

MAIN PICTURE This lively room has a retro vibe but the combination of pastels, primaries and off-white paintwork is undeniably contemporary.

INSET The pink chest of drawers – a revamped junkshop discovery – can easily be repainted in a few years if its young owner's tastes change.

key elements

Sleeping arrangements are the first consideration in any child's bedroom. Authentically vintage cots and beds do not meet modern safety requirements for babies and toddlers, but there are plenty of alternatives with which to create the look, including rush Moses baskets and oval cribs that convert into day beds. Save space with bunks for older siblings and pull-out trundle beds for sleepovers. Pretty antique single bedsteads – a favourite with young princesses – can be painted classic white, or with funkier vivid enamels.

A visit to any toyshop will confirm the fact that children revel in bright colours. The shabbiest bureau can be revived with a coat of paint and, as long as you keep to similar tones, furniture painted in a mixture of colours will look vibrant and exciting. You can add further layers of pattern with fabrics, but the inevitable accumulation of books, posters and building bricks will bring a kaleidoscope of colour in time. Fastidious parents, who prefer a more muted look, can try to keep this under control by planning ample storage. Old shop units with many drawers, shallow boxes for under the bed and high-level display shelving will all optimise space.

ABOVE, LEFT Every sleeping beauty needs her own fairytale chamber: this wooden hideaway has been built into the alcove beside a chimneybreast.
ABOVE, RIGHT Practical bunk beds maximise the floor area in this unfussy bedroom for two brothers.

RIGHT A giant pin board is an effective display solution. Copy the idea by stapling a remnant to a rectangle of soft board and securing it to the wall with picture plates. (Use magnetic boards as a spike-free alternative for small children.)

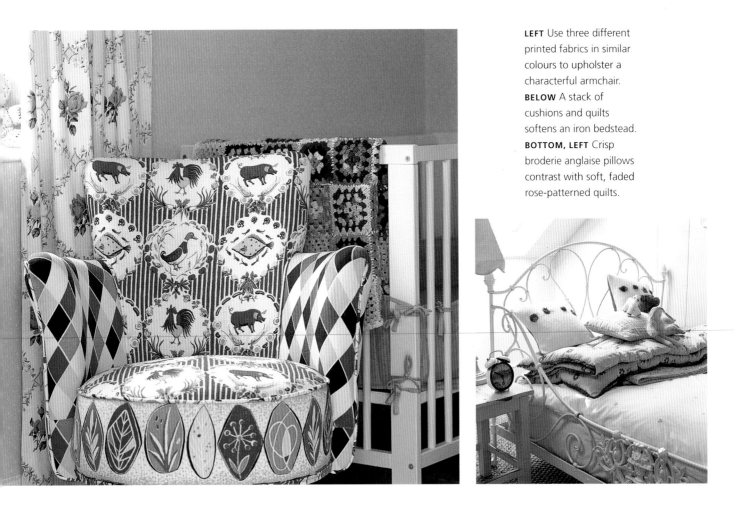

LEFT Use three different printed fabrics in similar colours to upholster a characterful armchair. **BELOW** A stack of cushions and quilts softens an iron bedstead. **BOTTOM, LEFT** Crisp broderie anglaise pillows contrast with soft, faded rose-patterned quilts.

fabrics

Whether you are looking for strong primaries or faded pastels to set the scene in a child's room, you will find plenty of vintage inspiration in shops selling both old and new textile pieces. If you search in the right places, there are still many original cotton curtains, bedspreads and dressing-table covers featuring prints of 1950s cowboys, racing cars and seaside scenes to be unearthed. Many of these designs are now being reproduced, as manufacturers follow the lead of Cath Kidston, the doyenne of vintage domesticity.

You may also find antique bedlinen, which has already been used by four generations but which still has much wear remaining. The smaller scale of children's bedding means that damaged sheets can be cut down and re-hemmed and, for the truly thrifty, offcuts can be stitched into cushion covers, tiny padded hearts or used in patchwork. Many old eiderdowns and quilts have survived as family heirlooms, but there also lots of new versions about, many hand-stitched in India, which will better withstand daily wear and tear.

Checked and striped fabrics, from any era and on every scale from pinstripe shirting to harlequin diamonds, are perennial favourites for children. They always look bright and cheerful, and can be mixed and matched with patterns or with florals to create a variety of themed looks from folk art to nautical.

MAIN PICTURE Ticking stripes and gingham checks in nautical red, white and blue would be ideal for either a boy's or girl's room. This colour scheme is one which will grow up with the child, as the soft toys are replaced with more sophisticated accessories.

FAR LEFT This woollen patchwork can be made very quickly. Edge each square with blanket stitch in contrasting tapestry yarn and join them together with slip stitch.
LEFT If you do not have a crocheter in the family, check out charity shops for bright afghan throws.

MATERIALS AND EQUIPMENT
selection of printed handkerchiefs
white bias binding
ric-rac braid
narrow gingham ribbon
decorative buttons
matching sewing thread
sewing kit

handkerchief curtain

The treasured collection of printed hankies I used to make this hand-stitched curtain dates back to my childhood in the 1970s. Boxed sets of seven, one for each day of the week, were popular gifts from my grandparents and great-aunts, who were anxious to encourage polite behaviour. The charming illustrations range from nursery rhyme characters and Mabel Lucie Attwell pixies to Bugs Bunny and Tweety Pie. (The bathroom curtain on page 63 was put together in a similar way.)

1 Wash and press the handkerchiefs, then lay them out on the floor to match the size and shape of the window, allowing an extra 15 cm (6 in) across the width to create a little fullness when the curtain is hung.

2 Line up whole handkerchiefs along the bottom edge, then trim others to size as necessary to give a straight top. Slip stitch them together (see page 101).

3 Slip stitch them together (see page 101), passing the needle through the existing hems to give an invisible seam. Join in vertical blocks, then sew the blocks together.

4 With right sides facing, pin and tack one edge of the bias binding to the curtain top along the crease. Fold it back over the raw edge, then tack and machine stitch down.

5 Pin, tack and hand-stitch a length of ric-rac over the binding.

6 For the ties, fold a 30 cm (12 in) length of ribbon in half and hand-stitch to the back of the bias binding at each join and at the two corners.

7 Trim the ends in fishtails and sew a button to the top edge at the base of each tie. Press, and then hang from a pole at the window.

finishing touches

Children are instinctive collectors, and feel reassured when surrounded by their favourite possessions. Make the most of this squirrelling habit by providing plenty of places for display, along with chests or boxes in which to keep prized keepsakes. Toys are meant to be played with, and if you have childhood mementos stowed away – a tattered teddy bear, a perambulator, toy fort or rocking horse – this is the place to show them off and share them with your own children. Hand-knitted or -crocheted animals and dolls enjoy almost cult status now and are often to be found at boot sales and flea markets, along with other vintage toys.

Tiny garments can be put out on view and displayed against the wall or on the back of the door. If space is at a premium, install two or more wooden peg rails beside the cot and hang up frocks, petticoats and home-made cardigans from small-sized hangers – this looks attractive and also means everything is to hand at getting up time. You can encourage imaginative play by keeping the family's unwanted clothes, hats and bags in a special place ready for dressing-up games, along with spare blankets, throws and lengths of cloth. Never forget that an ordinary pile of cushions may be used to construct a giant's castle and a rag rug can always turn into a flying carpet.

OPPOSITE ABOVE, FAR LEFT Make the most of your walls by clipping up artwork with clothes pegs screwed to lengths of wood and hanging dresses from peg rails.

OPPOSITE ABOVE, LEFT Tiny fingers enjoy playing with miniature collections – display them within the compartments of a paper-covered printer's tray.

OPPOSITE CENTRE, FAR LEFT Hang a row of sunhats from pegs all year round.

OPPOSITE CENTRE, LEFT A floppy-eared rabbit, made from a scrap of dress material, will be a lifelong friend.

OPPOSITE BELOW, FAR LEFT Scraps of bright stitchery cut from worn mats or napkins can be reused to make patchwork pieces.

OPPOSITE BELOW, LEFT This glamorous 1920s lady appears on the pages of a grown-up rag book.

THIS PAGE A unifying colour will always pull the look together. Here a pretty bedroom chair and a battered doll's pram share the same pale shell pink. The gilt-framed antique mirror is an elegant feature, much appreciated by a little girl with stylish tastes.

pull-along duck

This little white painted duck, which is made from a length of reclaimed floorboard, has a traditional charm that will appeal to all small children – and their parents. Once it is no longer played with, it is bound to become a special memento, to be treasured and passed on to the next generation.

MATERIALS AND EQUIPMENT

enough 1 cm (½ in) wood
to cut the following pieces:

two 13 cm x 19 cm (5 x 7½ in),
for body and head

one 17 x 9 cm (7 x 3½ in), for base

two 6 x 10 cm (2½ x 4 in), for wings

enough 8 mm (⅓ in) wood to make
four 5 cm (2 in) diameter circles,
for wheels

2 wooden buttons with
back loops, for eyes

1 large wooden bead for cord

wooden dowelling, for wing
and wheel dowels

10 cm (4 in) of 6 mm (¼ in)
30 cm (12 in) thick twine

tracing paper • pencil

G-cramps • jigsaw

drill with 6 mm (¼ in) and
2 mm (½₂ in) twist bits

medium and fine sandpaper

sanding block (optional)

scrap wood • ruler • screwdriver

wood glue • hammer

25 cm (10 in) shirring elastic

5 cm (2 in) No. 10 wood screw

NOTE This toy should not be given to a child under 36 months.

1 Trace the templates on page 103 and transfer all except the wheels on to the floorboard, remembering to include all the X-marks. Draw the wheels on the thin wood.

4 Make four X-marks on the edges of the long sides of the base, 3 cm (1¼ in) in from the ends. Holding the base secure with G-cramps, drill four 6 mm (¼ in) axle holes through the X- marks, 3 cm (1¼ in) into the base.

2 With G-cramps, attach the wood firmly to a workbench. Use a jigsaw to cut out all the shapes. Then, using a drill fitted with a 6 mm (¼ in) bit, make a hole through each wheel for the axle dowels.

3 Sand each shape with medium then fine sandpaper, rounding off all the corners and edges to achieve a smooth finish ready for painting. When sanding the flat surfaces, you may find it helpful to wrap the sandpaper around a sanding block.

5 Place a piece of scrap wood underneath the duck's body to protect your work surface and secure both pieces to the bench with G-cramps. Using a 2 mm (½₂ in) bit, drill holes at the X-mark through the head for the eyes, and through the centre of the body for the wings. Drill similar holes halfway through the thickness of the wings, on the inside. The pieces should now be painted before assembly (see page 103).

6 Paint all the shapes with one coat of white acrylic primer, then leave to dry for an hour. When dry, rub back with sandpaper to allow some of the grain to show through. Paint the base and the buttons for the eyes blue. Paint the wheels, beak and bead with cadmium orange. When dry, sand back each of the painted pieces to reveal some of the grain.

7 Cut a length of 2 mm (1/12 in) dowelling to fit through the body and halfway into each wing. Put a drop of glue into the drilled hole in the body, then carefully tap the dowel through with a hammer. Tap the wings on to the dowels so they fit snugly.

8 To make the eyes, knot the shirring elastic to the shank of one button, then thread the other end through the hole in the duck's head. Stretch the elastic and, maintaining the tension, tie it firmly to the other button. Trim the ends, apply glue to both button backs and release the elastic to hold the buttons securely in place.

9 To make the axles, cut the 6 mm (1/4 in) dowelling into four 6 cm (2 1/2 in) lengths, so that they fit into the holes in the base and through both wheels, leaving 2 cm (3/4 in) of dowel extending beyond each wheel. Paint blue and, when dry, drill a 2 mm (1/12 in) hole about 8 mm (1/3 in) from one end of each piece to take the wheel dowels. Put a little glue on the other end of each dowel, then tap them through the axle holes with a hammer. Slide a wheel on each. To make the wheel dowels, cut the remaining thin dowelling into four 1 cm (1/2 in) lengths and paint blue. When dry, glue one in each axle dowels to hold the wheels.

10 To secure the duck to the base, drill a hole up through the base, as marked. Then drill a smaller hole in the bottom of the duck to take the screw. Attach the base to the duck, using the large wood screw.

11 Drill a hole through the front of the base, as marked, to take the twine. Tie a knot in one end of the twine, thread the cord through the hole, then through the large bead. Tie a second knot at the other end of the twine to secure the bead. Apply a thin layer of glue to both knots to prevent them unravelling.

workrooms

Mundane tasks – arranging deliveries, paying bills, patching worn jeans – are an inevitable part of the daily routine and most households at least have a corner set aside for the sewing basket, phone directories and a row of filing boxes, if not a dedicated study. Modern communications, however, mean that additional space now has to be found for all the essential technology that goes with working from home, ordering online and doing homework. A vintage-style workroom should look like an integral part of your home, not an impersonal office full of bulky equipment and dull files, so stow your laptop away in a drawer and keep printers, scanners, faxes and sewing machines out of sight in cupboards or concealed behind a screen. You can then turn your attention to collecting and displaying the accessories and furniture that will create a lived-in, more congenial atmosphere for your working area.

key elements

Think laterally when planning a home workroom and utilise what you have to hand: any table can be used as a work surface, and woven shopping baskets or leather suitcases will house paperwork and stationery. If you prefer a more functional look, however, reclaimed and restored office furniture is easy to come by and adapts well to a domestic setting. Classic items like architect's plan chests and huge leather-topped partner's desks look great if you have the space, but smaller-scale writing tables and oak kneehole desks are equally attractive. Mid-twentieth-century metal desks, filing cabinets and lockers, reminiscent of civil service office suppliers, take on a cool, contemporary look when stripped of paint and polished to a dull sheen.

Well thought out lighting and supportive seating are important design elements if you are going to spend a long time writing, using a computer or sewing. There are plenty of old, new and reproduction desk lamps to choose from: the iconic anglepoise, first designed over 70 years ago, is still the most stylish of these. An authentic swivel chair is the perfect partner for a vintage desk, and sleeker than its modern counterpart... but you may need to place a cushion on the seat to add a little home comfort.

ABOVE, LEFT This well-planned homework area for an older child sits discreetly in a corner without dominating the bedroom. Now a design classic, the 1970s wall-mounted storage unit is the perfect way to keep stationery, keys, pencils and pens to hand without cluttering the desktop. The smooth curved shapes accentuate the functional lines of the desk and vintage yellow chair, while a bright-red desk light and an old record box add more primary colour to the neutral background.

BELOW, LEFT The filing cabinet, metal anglepoise desk lamp and old mesh wastepaper basket in this relaxed work space could have come straight from an office, but the battered wooden kitchen table, fresh flowers and quirky touches, such as the luggage labels tied on to the drawer handles, reveal the more homely setting. The table has been positioned within a bay window to make the most of the bright daylight and to provide a constantly changing view of the outside world.

LEFT A clever use of space in a loft conversion: the wide shelf directly under the dormer window acts as a desk, while the lower one provides plenty of extra storage.

MAIN PICTURE A splendid, vast filing cabinet, overhead lighting and a row of old office chairs, set on either side of a long refectory table, give a purposeful air to this design studio.

LEFT This wonderful old adjustable tailor's dummy is still put to its original use in a light-filled sewing room, but would look equally effective as an unusual display stand for favourite items of clothing, jewellery and hats.
BELOW, LEFT These ornamental hatboxes double up as storage containers for remnants of fabric. Arranged within an empty fireplace alcove, alongside a hand sewing machine and a basket of scraps, they provide an eye-catching focal point in a busy workroom.

fabrics

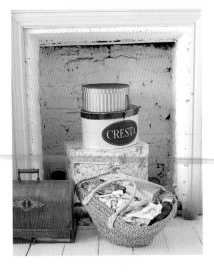

You do not have to be a textile artist or a dressmaker to enjoy collecting vintage fabrics and haberdashery: most people who enjoy needlework have their own personal hoard of materials, buttons, lace and ribbons, old silk scarves and embroidered napkins. Instead of storing these away in boxes, they can be put out on display in a sewing room or work area as a source of inspiration for future projects or just to be enjoyed for their unique qualities.

Glass-fronted draper's drawers are the perfect place to keep remnants and larger pieces of cloth, but these can also be folded and grouped together by colour, pattern or size, then stacked in wicker baskets or on open shelves. Clear jars, especially the larger ones, which once held sweets, make ideal containers for small scraps, buttons and beads. Professional designers will always have a 'mood board' as a source of inspiration in their studio, on which they pin favourite postcards, swatches, samples and lengths of braid and ribbons – a decorative idea that can be copied at home. Fabrics can also be used make a study or workroom less office-like. Make sure you have attractive curtains, covers and cushions surrounding you, and use flower-printed or striped offcuts or sample lengths to disguise dull files and notebooks.

TOP, LEFT A pretty flowered chintz slipcover will protect a well-loved but dog-eared novel from further wear and tear.

TOP, CENTRE Roll-up 'housewives' like this have been used for many years to store sewing scissors, buttons and needles. Make your own from a strip of flannel or fabric lined with silk and fitted with small pockets and tape loops in which to slot small items.

TOP, RIGHT This brocade drawstring pouch contains antique needlework tools: the Dorothy bag (on page 64) would also make a useful sewing-kit holder.

ABOVE, LEFT AND RIGHT Colourful pearl-headed pins are easier to use and prettier than plain steel dressmaker's pins.

LEFT Humble shoeboxes or purpose-made box files can be covered with remnants of floral fabric and displayed on shelves.

finishing touches

ABOVE, LEFT Fine hand writing has period charm: glue photocopied letters on to plain boxes and files.
ABOVE, CENTRE Turn plain writing paper into something special with simple details like these rows of pressed flowers.
ABOVE, RIGHT A length of silky ribbon and a drop pearl fastening add a touch of glamour.
BELOW, RIGHT Three antique wooden shoe lasts, screwed securely into the wall, make idiosyncratic hangers.
BELOW, LEFT A gold ribbon can be tied around a bundle of love letters.
LEFT, CENTRE The fastenings on these boxes are made from fine twine looped over linen buttons. The stamped numbers could easily be copied on to a pile of new boxes.
FAR RIGHT White-painted typesetters' drawers, with their many compartments, make good display cases.

Once you have settled on the furniture and soft furnishings for your sewing room or study, it is time to plan the final details. You will doubtless need some ordinary stationery supplies – ring binders, a calculator, a stapler and a hole puncher – which are essential but far from stimulating to look at, so these can be simply bundled away into interesting tote bags or carriers saved from your travels (as shown on the left) and hung up on the wall.

To complete the look, there are a few accessories that always evoke a traditional office environment. A round-faced schoolroom clock with large numerals, a wire mesh waste paper basket, a metal fan to keep you cool or a stack of wooden in-trays all have an authentic, hard-working appeal. A letter rack, like that on pages 88–89, is always useful and can be painted to match your room scheme or covered in photocopied manuscript to match the magazine file, opposite. Paintbrushes and pencils can be kept to hand on the desk in mugs or stoneware jars and, if you really want to return to a less frenetic age, you could buy a reconditioned vintage telephone, a blotting pad, a fountain pen and a bottle of ink.

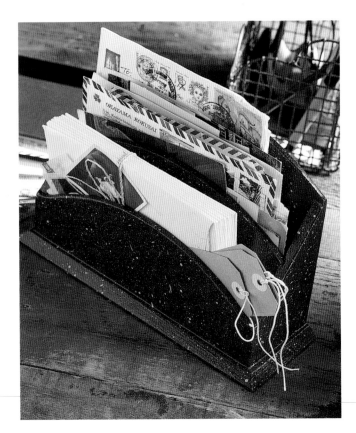

letter rack
A useful aid to keeping track of your correspondence, Sally and Stewart Walton's rack has separate compartments for both incoming and outgoing letters. It is made out of fibreboard, with a wooden bead trim around the base.

1 Enlarge the templates on page 103 and transfer the shapes on to the MDF. Clamp the wood to a workbench using G-cramps. Wearing a face mask, cut each shape out carefully with a jigsaw, and then sand any rough edges.

MATERIALS AND EQUIPMENT

enough 6 mm (¼ in) MDF to cut the following pieces:

one 7.3 x 23 cm (2⅞ x 9⅛ in), for front

one 15.5 x 23 cm (6⅛ x 9⅛ in), for back

one 11 x 21.8 cm (4⅜ x 8⅝ in), for central divider

two 15.5 x 7 cm (6⅛ x 2¾ in), for sides

one approximately 23 x 8.2 cm (9⅛ x 3¼ in) for base (cut to fit)

60 cm (24 in) length of 1.5 cm (⅝ in) triangular beading, to surround front and sides of base

tracing paper · pencil

G-cramps · workbench

face mask · jigsaw

medium and fine sandpaper

wood glue · panel pins · hammer

tenon saw · mitre box

2 To assemble the rack, apply wood glue to the edges of the side pieces and butt them up to the back and front pieces. Clamp these joints until the glue has bonded, then reinforce with panel pins tapped through from the front and back into the sides.

3 Place the assembled rack on the MDF and draw round the bottom edge. Cut out the base around this line (wearing the mask), apply wood glue to the bottom edge of the rack and clamp it in position. Pin through from underneath to reinforce.

4 Mark the position of the central divider on the side pieces. Apply wood glue to the side and bottom edges and slip it in place (see opposite).

5 Using a tenon saw, cut three lengths of beading to fit snugly around the front and sides of the base, mitring the corners at 45 degrees with a mitre box.

6 Glue the beading in position, placing the rack on a flat surface so that the base is level. Clamp in position until the glue has bonded.

PAINT PALETTE AND EQUIPMENT

white acrylic primer

artists' acrylic paints in the following colours:

chocolate brown

Venetian red • ultramarine

black • white • grey

water-based satin varnish

shallow white container, for mixing

broad long-handled paintbrush

cardboard box, for spray-booth

stiff-bristled paintbrush

varnishing brush

Paint swatches

Chocolate brown

Venetian red

Blue-black (optional)
  3 parts ultramarine
  1 part black

Pink
  3 parts Venetian red
  1 part white

Grey
  3 parts grey
  1 part ultramarine

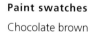

Steps to paint

1 Paint the whole rack with white acrylic primer, using a broad long-handled paintbrush to get down into the divisions. Leave to dry.

2 Again using a long-handled brush, apply the chocolate brown base coat and let it dry.

3 Make a simple three-sided spray-booth out of a large cardboard box.

4 Practise your spattering technique on scrap paper: load the stiff-bristled paintbrush with paint, then run your finger across the top to flick dots of paint on to the surface. Some dots will be bigger than others, but try not to make them too big or the paint will run and spoil the effect. Flick first with Venetian red, then with a blue-black, if you decide to use it, then with pink, and finally with grey. Leave to dry.

5 When you are satisfied with the overall effect, apply two coats of water-based satin varnish according to the manufacturer's instructions.

outdoors

Despite the vagaries of the climate, outdoor life is increasingly popular and the boundaries between house and garden often become blurred during the summer months. The garden is no longer just a place to hang out the washing or grow vegetables: spaces from orchards and overgrown lawns to urban backyards have been transformed into relaxed living areas where we can laze, dine, play and just enjoy looking at the trees, plants and wildlife.

Always informal and individual, contemporary vintage style works particularly well outdoors. Faded chintz, long-used garden furniture, squashy cushions and patchwork quilts look at home amid lush green foliage and scented flowers. Authentic garden antiques are comparatively rare and not always in the best condition, so look out for affordable reproductions or give a distressed finish to new pieces – this is the perfect place to mix old and new.

key elements

Garden furniture is essential for *alfresco* eating and socialising, and there are many old and vintage-style tables and chairs, in both wood and metal, from which to choose. Genuine antiques, with attractively weathered or distressed surfaces, have survived many years of use and blend well with the natural textures of wooden fencing, stone terraces or brick walls. If you are buying new furniture, painted wood will inevitably peel if left out for long enough, whilst benches made from reddish-brown hardwoods fade to a silvery grey in time.

Architectural salvage yards are a good hunting ground for furniture and also other horticultural items such as cold frames, wrought iron gates, metal rollers and cloches, which may be put to their original purpose, or treated as objets d'art. If you want to create hard landscaping within the garden, try cladding walls or patios with reclaimed paving slabs, granite sets and slate tiles. Authentic garden statuary and hand-thrown terracotta pots are sought after and expensive. Cast concrete or terracotta reproductions will become encrusted with lichens and moss in time, but you can always imitate the ageing process with a coat of dilute white or coloured emulsion paint.

ABOVE, LEFT A row of large colour-washed terracotta plant pots, spilling over with pelargoniums, has been arranged on a low wall, where it casts shade across a secluded work space and makes an informal divider between indoors and outdoors.
ABOVE, RIGHT Old tools are too interesting to be consigned to the back of the potting shed. Galvanised watering cans and containers, a sieve, trowels, forks and even a birdhouse appeal to the armchair gardener as well as the green-fingered.
LEFT The original faded blue paintwork on these louvre shutters, the scuffed planks and the old wooden chair set off the adjacent urn.

MAIN PICTURE Remove old paintwork from vintage furniture with chemical stripper, a scraper and a wire brush, then rub down with wire wool before repainting.

RIGHT The mesh seats of these sinuous chairs were designed so water drains easily. They can be left outdoors all year round, but metal furniture needs special attention.

THIS PICTURE Improvise a sun canopy for a day bed by stringing spare sheets or lengths of billowing sheer fabric between a tree and a bamboo pole.

ABOVE, LEFT The muted tones of this rose-printed cushion, quilt and knitted throw seem to merge into their green environment.

ABOVE, CENTRE To measure up for these quilted pads add 10 cm (4 in) to the dimensions of the seat, then make a cushion as on page 101.

ABOVE, RIGHT For this engaging peg bag, cut and bind an opening across a child's jersey, seam the bottom and insert a small hanger.

BELOW Lounging in a hammock is the epitome of summer ease – make yourself even snugger with plenty of cushions and a quilt.

fabrics

Look to your surroundings and take nature as your inspiration when selecting textiles for outside spaces. Strong colours and bold shapes look at home by the sea or in a sun-drenched back yard, whilst sprigged florals echo the varied planting and dappled green shade of a country plot. All soft furnishings take on a more informal appearance when they are put outside, so use them to add comfort and individuality to your garden.

Dress up old metal chairs with flowery seat pads and drape a matching cloth over a garden table to set the scene for lunch. Folding wooden seating – deckchairs or director's chairs – can be given an aged look by replacing the existing slings with vintage-style fabric, cut and seamed to the same size. Repaint the framework to match. Lay a quilt over a plastic dust sheet pile it with cushions and then picnic or just stretch out on the lawn. Parasols, awnings and canopies all provide welcome shade and are usually made from weather-resistant acrylic cloth, specially designed for outdoor use. Soften the look by re-covering or draping them with patterned remnants, but remember that the sun will fade (and dampness will rot) any fabrics left out for too long.

finishing touches

TOP, LEFT Polka-dot ceramic tumblers make a colourful alternative to ordinary flowerpots for these bright-yellow marigolds.

TOP, RIGHT A mid-twentieth-century design classic, this white-painted wire chair by Harry Bertoia brings 1950s style to a suburban garden.

CENTRE, LEFT Plant stands and baskets fashioned from ornately woven wirework were immensely popular in Victorian gardens and conservatories; see how to make your own simplified version in the project overleaf.

CENTRE, RIGHT This somewhat startled pottery hen has been given a new purpose as a plant holder.

BELOW, LEFT Another imaginative reuse of an old container: a stencilled hot-water jug holds a pretty verbena.

BELOW, RIGHT Any design motif becomes more effective when repeated. Here, a row of four 'brown betty' teapots makes a strong impact on a weathered windowsill.

OPPOSITE, ABOVE RIGHT Keep an eye out for old wooden storage crates with stencilled lettering.

OPPOSITE, BELOW LEFT Although your garden may be full of flowering plants, a handful of cut stems will always add extra interest to the table.

OPPOSITE, BELOW RIGHT A functional old galvanised bucket serves as a useful garden trug.

As outdoor living is redefined, gardens and patios have become open-air extensions, to be decorated with the same care and attention as an interior. Whatever its size, there will always be room for the quirky items that give character and individuality. In addition to displaying old equipment, such as cloches, propagating trays and splendidly dented watering cans or imported olive jars and amphorae, this is the place to recycle domestic items that are no longer suitable for daily use. Think laterally: anything from a lidless coffee pot or a cracked jug to a plastic shopping tote can double up as a container: simply add drainage and compost, then fill with plants. At night time you can set the scene for a romantic dinner by hanging up strings of outdoor fairy lights, insect-repellent citronella candles, shadow lanterns or simple tea lights in empty glass jam jars – and keep yourself warm with a fashionable chimenea fireplace or café-style gas heaters.

wirework basket
This wirework basket by Jane Seabrook is more of an enclosure than a container; such edgings were used in the early nineteenth century as a feature surround for garden plants. A strip of galvanised iron, bent into a circle, creates the framework for the miniature fence that supports the bushes. The best roses to use are low-growing ground cover varieties, but you can adapt the size of the planter to accommodate larger shrub roses. Be sure to wear protective gloves when making this project.

MATERIALS AND EQUIPMENT

1 sheet of galvanised iron, 120 x 30 cm (48 x 12 in) use a gauge than can be cut with tin snips

6 galvanised roofing bolts, 1 cm (½ in) long and 6 mm (¼ in) wide

23 m (25 yd) of 5 mm (⅛ in) thick galvanised fencing wires

50 x 35 cm (20 x 14 in) rectangle of 2.5 cm (1 in) plywood tin snips

hacksaw and vice or G-cramps

jigsaw

grey-blue metal primer

well-rotted manure and rose fertiliser

5 bare-root rose plants (*Rosa* 'The Fairy')

Making the basket

1 Cut the sheet of iron into 10 cm (4 in) wide strips, two at 120 cm (48 in) long and one at 60 cm (24 in) long.

2 Drill two 7 mm (⅜ in) diameter holes in the same positions at the ends of each strip. Fix the three sections together to form a ring by lining up the holes and securing the joins with roofing bolts. This strip acts as a template for preparing the bed and as a retainer for the basket.

3 For the basket, cut the fencing wire into sixteen 140 cm (55 in) lengths with a hacksaw. Use a vice or G-cramp to hold the wire in place when cutting.

4 To shape the wire you will need to make a former from the plywood; this will act as a solid template around which to bend one into shape. Mark the top centre point and draw the curved sides to within 20 cm (8 in) of the base. Cut out the shape with a jigsaw.

5 Mark the centre point on each length of fencing wire. Using a vice, bend the wire at this point into a right angle: you may find a lump hammer useful.

6 Place this right angle over the point of the former and bend the wire to fit the template exactly. The wire should extend for about 10 cm (4 in) beyond the lower edge of the former.

7 Each section of the planter now needs to be bent outwards in a curve. Turn the arches sideways and use the former to guide the curve in to shape.

8 Before constructing the basket, paint all the metal components with metal primer. The grey blue used here appears as a patinated copper colour and provides a good foil for the pink roses.

Preparing and planting the bed

9 Choose an area of flat ground for your rose bed. If the area is grassed over, position the ring and cut around its inner edge to mark the turf. Put the ring aside and remove the turf by dividing it into squares and lifting out with a spade. Turn over the bed and fork in the manure, and then gently press the ring into position.

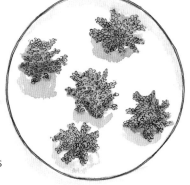

10 Plant the five roses, positioning them according the planting plan (right). Make sure the junction of stem and root are at surface level. Top dress with rose fertiliser.

Assembling the basket

11 Insert the first wire arch hard up against the inner edge of the ring with the tip bending outwards and push it about 15–20 cm (6–8 in) into the ground. Position the next arch so that it overlaps the first one by half its width. Repeat this process for the remaining arches all the way round the circumference of the ring; you may need to adjust the spacing on some of the wires for a neat and even fit.

12 Secure the basket sections together by twisting lengths of thin galvanised wire around the crossover junctions on each arch.

13 Prune the roses to that they form a slightly domed shape, and trim back any grass around the outer edge for a formal effect.

Alternative planting schemes

Try the roses 'White Pet' or 'Nozomi' for a container of this size or, for a larger arrangement, use the pink rose 'Marguerite Hilling' or its creamy-white sister 'Nevada'. A suitable flowering shrub would be *Camellia japonica* 'Alba Plena'.

techniques

SEWING KIT

The equipment and haberdashery needed for most needlework is minimal, but it is worth investing in the best tools to help you achieve lasting and professional results.

Modern sewing machines have many advanced features, but the projects in this book require only a basic straight stitch and a zigzag for neatening seams. It is useful to have several pairs of scissors, each with its own purpose, such as dressmaking shears, paper scissors and embroidery scissors. Your sewing box should also contain a selection of needles, a thimble, dressmaker's pins and a fading or water-soluble dressmaker's pen for transferring marks.

SEAMS AND HEMS

If you can hem the edges of a length of fabric and join two pieces together, you have mastered the basic techniques of sewing and should be able to tackle all of the step-by-step projects described in the earlier chapters.

1 Plain seam

The extra fabric needed to join two edges is given as the seam allowance. To keep the seam consistent, match the raw edges to the corresponding line on the machine's baseplate when stitching. With right sides facing, line up the two edges and pin at 5–10 cm (2–4 in) intervals. Tack, then machine stitch along the seam line. Unpick the tacking, then press the seam open or over to one side, as directed.

2 Neatened seam

Raw fabric edges may fray, especially if an item is washed, but this can be prevented by neatening the seam. If it is to be pressed open, zigzag or overlock each cut edge before seaming. If the seam is to be pressed to one side, the allowance can be trimmed and the two edges zigzagged together (as shown left).

1

3

3 Sewing round a corner

Stitch to the end of the seam allowance and, keeping the needle down, raise the presser foot. Turn the fabric through 90 degrees and continue sewing. Clip off the corner to within 3 mm (⅛ in) of the stitching before turning through so that it will lie flat.

2

4 Double hem

This consists of one narrow and one deeper turning or two equal-sized turnings (which give a firmer edge to finer fabrics). Press the two folds under and pin, then tack in place. Machine stitch close to the inner fold or finish by hand with slip stitch (see 7, opposite) if you do not want the stitching to show on the right side.

4

5

5 Curved seam

The allowance on a curved join has to be trimmed back to 1 cm (½ in) and clipped so that the seam will lie flat. On an outside curve make small notches. On an inside curve, snip a short distance into the allowance at regular intervals.

6 Mitred corner

When two hems meet at right angles, the surplus fabric is neatened with a mitre to avoid bulk. Press the turnings under, then unfold. Fold each corner inwards and press so the creases line up to make a square (as shown). Refold the hems, then slip stitch the folded edges together (see left). For a double hem, unfold the second turning only before refolding and stitching.

7 Slip stitch

Slip stitch is used for joining two folded edges where they meet, for example, at a mitred corner or along the opening of a simple cushion cover, and also to secure a double hem. Bring the needle out through the fold and pick up two threads of the other fabric on the other side with the point. Pass the needle back through the first fold for 6 mm (¼ in) and repeat to the end.

CUSHIONS AND PILLOWS

Ready-made pads to go inside cushions or pillows, with feather or synthetic fillings, come in a range of shapes and many sizes.

1 Basic cushion cover

The simplest covers are closed with slip stitch. This has to be unpicked and resewn for cleaning, but it is almost invisible, especially if the seams are piped. Covers should be the same dimensions as the pad, without any extra seam allowance, to give the cushion a well-stuffed look. Cut two pieces of fabric the same size as the pad. Add piping if required, then pin and tack the edges together with right sides facing. Machine stitch, leaving a 25 cm (10 in) gap along one side. Clip the corners, turn right side out and press. Press under the unstitched seam allowance. Insert the pad and slip stitch the opening with matching thread.

2 Buttoned fastenings

If you want to add a row of buttons to an envelope back, the opening will need to be reinforced, so allow a 5 cm (2 in) double hem along each edge (see opposite). Mark the button positions along the centre of one hem and make matching vertical buttonholes on the other panel by hand or by machine. Make up the cover as described in 1, pinning on the buttonhole panel first, then sew on the buttons.

templates

The outlines shown below have all been reduced in size
so they fit on these pages. To make them the correct size,
enlarge them on a photocopier by the percentages given.

ETHEREAL THROW
(page 20) Enlarge by 175%

PULL-ALONG DUCK
(page 78)
Enlarge by 145%

PAINT PALETTE AND
EQUIPMENT

white acrylic primer

artists' acrylic paints in
the following colours:

brilliant blue

white

cadmium orange

shallow white container,
for mixing

10 mm artist's brush

Paint swatches

Blue
    3 parts brilliant blue
    1 part white

Cadmium orange

BODY & HEAD
cut 2

WING
cut 2

WHEEL
cut 4

BASE
cut 1

LETTER RACK (page 88)
Enlarge by 170%

BACK
cut 1

CENTRAL DIVIDER
cut 1

FRONT
cut 1

SIDE
cut 2

sources

BAILEYS
Whitecross Farm
Bridstow
Herefordshire HR9 6JU
t. 01989 563015
www.baileyshomeandgarden.co.uk
*Everything including the kitchen sink: new
and salvaged glamorous hardware, vintage
mirrors, retro light switches, dress forms
and lighting.*

THE BLUE DOOR
74 Church Road
London SW13 0DQ
t. 020 8748 9785
www.thebluedoor.co.uk
*Reproduction Gustavian painted furniture,
plus fabrics, lighting and accessories.*

CABBAGES AND ROSES
3 Langton Street
London SW10 0JL
t. 020 7352 7333
*New retro fabrics and gingham by the
metre or made into napkins, covered box
files, shower caps, duvet covers and
cushions.*

CAROLINE ZOOB
Shop A, 33 Cliffe High Street Lewes
East Sussex BN7 2AN
t. 01273 476464
www.carolinezoob.com
*Hand-made and antique collectables,
including cushions and pictures made from
antique textiles, painted china, vintage
blankets, patchwork quilts and decorative
antiques.*

CATH KIDSTON
t. 020 7935 6555
www.cathkidston.co.uk
*The designer who launched a look:
revamped nostalgic florals and children's
prints in bright new colours, tinware, china
and sewing products.*

CHANDLERS
t. 0870 240 1123
*Traditional enamel kitchenware in
contemporary pastel colours, striped
Cornishware, linen hand towels and tea
towels amongst other treasures.*

CLASSIC QUILTS
The Old Bakery
Charlton Marshall
Blandford Forum
Dorset DT11 9NH
t. 01258 453913
*Hand-crafted quilts in a variety of patterns
and sizes.*

FAIR & WEATHERED
Ringwood, New Road
Brighstone
Isle of Wight PO30 4BP
t. 07979 593096
*Vintage furniture and accessories for home
and garden from across the globe.*

FARROW & BALL
Uddens Estate, Wimborne
Dorset BH21 7NL
t. 01202 876141
www.farrow-ball.co.uk
*Paint and wallpaper made using
traditional methods.*

FRENCH COLLECTABLES
Church View House
26 High Street
Bushey WD23 3HL
t. 020 8950 0930
www.frenchcollectables.com
*Unusual, characterful and sometimes rare
French antiques for the home.*

FOUND
t. 0870 166 8231
www.foundat.co.uk
*Beautiful discoveries by post including
traditional tin and wooden toys.*

GARDEN REQUISITES
t. 01225 859908
www.garden-requisites.co.uk
*Bespoke traditional wirework, inspired by
Georgian originals: porticos, arches, plant
trainers and arbours.*

GOOSEBERRY TART
Pigeons Piece, Horseshoe Lane
Wootton by Woodstock
Oxon OX20 1DR
t. 01993 810681
www.gooseberrytart.com
*Antique and collectable kitchenalia, plus
knitted tea cosies, kitchen fairies and
aprons, and cushions made from vintage
and reproduction fabric.*

GRAND ILLUSIONS
41 Crown Road
St Margarets
Twickenham
Middx TW1 3EJ
www.grandillusions.co.uk
*Vintage living meets new country,
including zinc watering cans, buckets and
pot holders*

INSIDE OUTDOORS
The North Lodge
London Minstead
Hampshire SO43 7FT
t. 07909 522727
www.insideoutdoors.com
*Unique and individual furnishings and
accessories for the home and garden.*

JANE SACCHI
www.janesacchi.com
*Wonderful new heavy blue, white and
natural linen woven in traditional style.*

LABOUR AND WAIT
18 Cheshire Street
London E2 6EH
t. 020 7729 6253
www.labourandwait.co.uk
Timeless products for the home and garden, which celebrate functional design: hardware, feather dusters, wonderful brushes and children's classics.

LIVING VINTAGE
113d Northcote Road
London SW11 6PN
t. 020 7223 4440
Antique quilts and eiderdowns, cushions, pictures and scented gifts.

LOUISE LOVES
19 Stanley Street
Southport
Merseyside PR9 0BY
t. 01704 538606
www.louiseloves.co.uk
Vintage and vintage-inspired fabrics, lighting, quilts, blankets and kitchenalia.

MELIN TREGWYNT
Tregwynt Mill
Castlemorris
Haverfordwest
Pembrokeshire SQ62 5UX
t. 01348 891225
www.melintregwynt.co.uk
Welsh woollen blankets, throws and cushions that can now be seen in the hippest hotels and coolest rooms.

THE OLD POTTING SHED
t. 0118 933 1510
www.thevintagelook.co.uk
Vintage-style home accessories, including enamelware and wirework.

STEVE HANDLEY
24 Rushworth Avenue
West Bridgeford
Nottingham NG2 7LF
t. 0115 982 0427
www.stevehandley.co.uk
Cupboards, dressers, chairs, tables, beds and hooks made from reclaimed timber and found objects.

LONDON MARKETS

Most street markets have a few bric-à-brac stalls, but here is a list of established locations specializing in antiques and second-hand items. Consult websites for seasonal opening hours. For general information on street markets in London, visit www.streetsensation.co.uk/markets.

PORTOBELLO
Portobello Road, London W11
Friday and Saturday, 8am to 5pm
www.portobelloroad.co.uk

BRICK LANE
Brick Lane, Cheshire Street and
Sclater Street, London E1 and E2
Sunday, 6am to 1pm
www.eastlondonmarkets.com

BERMONDSEY
Bermondsey Square, London SE1
Friday, 5am to 1pm

CAMDEN
Camden High Street, London NW1
Saturday and Sunday, 9am to 5pm,
and most weekdays
www.camdenlock.net

GREENWICH
Greenwich Church Street, Stockwell Street and Greenwich High Road, London SE10
Saturday and Sunday, 9.30am to 5pm
www.greenwich-market.co.uk

OUTSIDE LONDON
Among regular antique fairs are those at Newark (Notts), Swinderby (Lincs), Ardingly (East Sussex) and Goodwood (West Sussex). Consult the following websites for more information: www.antiques-atlas.com and www.artefact.co.uk.

AROUND EUROPE

For general information on flea markets and a comprehensive list of links, consult www.fleamarket.com.

FRANCE
www.discoverfrance.net

PUCES DE CLIGNANCOURT
Rue des Entrepots, Saint Ouen
75018 Paris
Saturday, Sunday, Monday
www.parispuces.com

PUCES DE MONTREUIL
Avenue de la Porte de Montreuil
75020 Paris
Saturday, Sunday, Monday.

BELGIUM
For information on antiques and flea markets in Belgium, consult www.visitbelgium.com.

DENMARK
For information on flea markets, auction houses and antiques in Copenhagen and surrounding areas, visit www.woko.dk. Another good site for second-hand shops and flea markets is www.useit.dk.

THE NETHERLANDS
The Netherlands' largest second-hand event is on 30 April, when the whole of Amsterdam turns into one huge flea market! The areas of Noordermarkt and Waterlooplein also host regular good markets – visit tourist offices in the city or look on the internet for details.

index

picture credits

Key: ph=photographer, il=illustrator, a=above, b=below, r=right, l=left, c=centre.

Endpapers Sandra Lane/cushions and throw from Cath Kidston; 1 ph Polly Wreford/Emma Greenhill's London home; 2 ph Catherine Gratwicke/Martin Barrell & Amanda Sellers' home, owners of Maisonette, London; 3 ph Debi Treloar/the home of Patty Collister in London, owner of An Angel At My Table; 4 ph Sandra Lane/the home of Patty Collister in London, owner of An Angel At My Table-cushions and throws vintage Cath Kidston at An Angel At My Table; 5 ph Tom Leighton; 6l ph Debi Treloar/the guesthouse of the interior designer & artist Philippe Guilmin, Brussels; 6c ph Debi Treloar /author, stylist and 'Caravan' (shop) owner Emily Chalmers and director Chris Richmond's home in London; 6r ph Debi Treloar; 7l ph Caroline Arber/designed and made by Jane Cassini and Ann Brownfield; 7c ph Polly Wreford; 7r ph Tom Leighton; 8l ph Caroline Arber; 8c ph Catherine Gratwicke/Caroline Zoob's workroom; 8r ph David Loftus; 9l ph Polly Wreford; 9c ph Caroline Arber; 9r ph Sandra Lane; 10 ph Polly Wreford/Ros Fairman's house in London; 11l ph Caroline Arber/designed and made by Jane Cassini and Ann Brownfield; 11c ph Polly Wreford/Emma Greenhill's London home; 11r ph Polly Wreford /Adria Ellis' apartment in New York; 12a both ph Debi Treloar/Mark and Sally of Baileys Home and Garden's house in Herefordshire; 12b ph Polly Wreford/Mary Foley's house in Connecticut; 13 ph Catherine Gratwicke/Laura Stoddart's apartment in London; 14 ph Debi Treloar/Anna Massee of Het Grote Avontuur (The Great Adventure)'s home in Amsterdam; 15al ph Debi Treloar/the home of Studio Aandacht, design by Ben Lambers; 15ar ph Catherine Gratwicke/Lulu Guinness's home in London; 15b ph Polly Wreford/Emma Greenhill's London home; 16a ph Catherine Gratwicke/Francesca Mills' house in London-70s scarf cushions from Maisonette; 16b ph Catherine Gratwicke/Lucy and Marc Salem's London home-striped chair by Lucy Salem; 17al ph Sandra Lane/the home of Patty Collister in London, owner of An Angel At My Table-square cushions from An Angel At My Table, bag by Cath Kidston at An Angel At My Table; 17ac ph Debi Treloar/designer Petra Boase & family's home in Norfolk; 17ar ph Sandra Lane/Karen Nicol and Peter Clark's home in London-cushion made by Karen Nicol; 17b ph Catherine Gratwicke/Lulu Guinness's home in London; 18a ph Catherine Gratwicke/the home of Patty Collister in London, owner of An Angel At My Table; 18bl ph Sandra Lane/cushions made by Karen Nicol; 18br ph Catherine Gratwicke/vintage floral cushions with velvet flowers by Lucy Salem; 18–19 ph Debi Treloar/designer Susanne Rützou's home in Copenhagen; 19ac&bc ph Debi Treloar/Debi Treloar's home in London; 19ar ph Debi Treloar/the Chestnut Hill home of Pamela Falk; 19br ph Caroline Arber/designed and made by Jane Cassini and Ann Brownfield; 20–21 ph Sandra Lane, il Lizzie Sanders/Karen Nicol and Peter Clark's home in London–cushions and throw by Karen Nicol; 22–23 ph Sandra Lane, il Lizzie Sanders/cushions by Lucinda Ganderton; 24 ph Debi Treloar; 25al ph Catherine Gratwicke; 25ar ph Polly Wreford/Karen Nicol and Peter Clark's home in London; 25c,cr&bl ph Debi Treloar; 25br Polly Wreford; 26al ph Catherine Gratwicke; 26ac ph Catherine Gratwicke/Lulu Guinness's home in London; 26ar ph Caroline Arber/designed and made by Jane Cassini and Ann Brownfield; 26bl ph Catherine Gratwicke; 26br ph David Loftus; 27 main ph Catherine Gratwicke/Lulu Guinness's home in London; 27 inset ph Debi Treloar/designer Petra Boase & family's home in Norfolk; 28 ph Catherine Gratwicke/Claudia Bryant's house in London-apron made by Emily Medley; 29l ph Catherine Gratwicke/Laura Stoddart's apartment in London; 29c ph David Brittain; 29r ph Debi Treloar/the guesthouse of the interior designer & artist Philippe Guilmin, Brussels; 30al ph David Brittain/kitchen designed and supplied by Cunningham Furniture; 30ar ph Debi Treloar/Annelie Bruijn's home in Amsterdam; 30b ph Debi Treloar/Anna Massee of Het Grote Avontuur (The Great Adventure)'s home in Amsterdam; 31 ph Debi Treloar/Cristine Tholstrup Hermansen and Helge Drenck's house in Copenhagen; 32al ph Christopher Drake/Enrica Stabile's house in Brunello; 32ar ph Catherine Gratwicke/Rose Hammick's home in London; 32b Rose Hammick's home in London; 33al&ac ph Caroline Arber/designed and made by Jane Cassini and Ann Brownfield; 33ar ph Catherine Gratwicke/pan holder made by Lattika Jain; 33cr ph Debi Treloar; 33b all ph David Loftus; 34–35 ph Catherine Gratwicke, il Lizzie Sanders/Claudia Bryant's house in London-apron made by Emily Medley; 36al ph Catherine Gratwicke/felt place mats made by Sasha Gibb, egg-cosies made by Cecilie Telle; 36ac ph Sandra Lane; 36ar ph Polly Wreford; 36bl ph Debi Treloar; 36br ph Catherine Gratwicke; 37 ph Debi Treloar/designer Susanne Rützou's home in Copenhagen; 38al ph Catherine Gratwicke/Lesley Dilcock's house in London; 38ar ph Tom Leighton; 38b ph Catherine Gratwicke/Martin Barrell & Amanda Sellers' home, owners of Maisonette, London; 39a ph Catherine Gratwicke/Lulu Guinness's home in London; 39bl ph Caroline Arber/designed and made by Jane Cassini and Ann Brownfield; 39bc&br ph Sandra Lane; 40–41 ph James Merrell, il Helen Smythe; 42 ph Alan Williams/the Norfolk home of Geoff & Gilly Newberry of Bennison Fabrics – fabric on wall Bennison's Daisy Chain; 43l ph Debi Treloar/designer Petra Boase & family's home in Norfolk; 43c ph Debi Treloar; 43r ph Polly Wreford; 44a ph Catherine Gratwicke/Rose Hammick's home in London; 44b ph Catherine Gratwicke/the home of Patty Collister in London, owner of An Angel At My Table-dressing table from An Angel At My Table, curtain from Lucy Salem; 45a ph Debi Treloar/Mark and Sally of Baileys Home and Garden's house in Herefordshire; 45b ph Debi Treloar/designer Petra Boase & family's home in Norfolk; 46–47 ph James Merrell, il Lizzie Sanders/voile from Osborne & Little, lining from Designers Guild; 48al ph Sandra Lane/vintage throw courtesy of Karen Nicol; 48ar ph Sandra Lane/pillowcase from J&M Davidson, lavender bag from Graham & Green; 48b all ph Sandra Lane; 49al ph Chris Everard/fashion designer Carla Saibene's home in Milan; 49ar ph Debi Treloar/the Philadelphia home of Kristin Norris, creative director at Anthropologie and Trevor Lunn, digital designer; 49b ph Catherine Gratwicke/Rose Hammick's home in London; 50al ph Catherine Gratwicke/retro laundry bags from The Laundry; 50ac ph Catherine Gratwicke; 50bl ph Catherine Gratwicke/lavender bag from Susannah, retro bedlinen from the Laundry; 50bc ph Catherine Gratwicke/patchwork bag made from antique quilts and ticking by Sue Holley of Susannah in

Bath; **50–51** ph Catherine Gratwicke/Lesley Dilcock's house in London; **51a** ph Caroline Arber/designed and made by Jane Cassini and Ann Brownfield; **51bl** ph Catherine Gratwicke; **51br** Rose Hammick's home in London–patchwork quilt by Emily Medley; **52–53** ph David Montgomery, il Lizzie Sanders/Blakes Lodging designed by Jeanie Blake www.picket.com/blakesBB/blakes.htm, throw by Jeanie Blake; **54a** all ph David Brittain; **54bl** ph Caroline Arber/designed and made by Jane Cassini and Ann Brownfield; **54br** ph Sandra Lane; **55a** ph Catherine Gratwicke/Lucy and Marc Salem; **55cl** ph Debi Treloar/designer Susanne Rützou's home in Copenhagen; **55cr** ph Catherine Gratwicke; **55bl** ph Debi Treloar/Anna Massee of Het Grote Avontuur (The Great Adventure)'s home in Amsterdam; **55br** ph Catherine Gratwicke/interior designer Sue West's house in Gloucestershire; **56–57** ph Sandra Lane, il Lizzie Sanders/cushions made by Karen Nicol; **58** ph Chris Everard/Lulu Guinness's home in London; **59l&r** ph Chris Everard; **59c** ph Catherine Gratwicke; **60al** ph Debi Treloar/designer Petra Boase & family's home in Norfolk; **60ar** ph Tom Leighton; **60b** ph Debi Treloar/the guesthouse of the interior designer & artist Philippe Guilmin, Brussels; **61 main** ph Tom Leighton; **61** inset ph Caroline Arber/Hoggy & Mark Nicholl's home in Wiltshire; **62 main** ph Polly Wreford; **62** inset ph Debi Treloar/the home of Patty Collister in London, owner of An Angel At My Table; **63bl** ph Debi Treloar; **63al** ph Catherine Gratwicke/Claudia Bryant's house in London-vintage fabric-lined towel from Lucy Salem; **63ar** ph Debi Treloar/the Chestnut Hill home of Pamela Falk; **63br** ph Catherine Gratwicke/Lucy and Marc Salem's London home; **64–65** ph Catherine Gratwicke, il Lizzie Sanders/designer Caroline Zoob's home in East Sussex-floral Dorothy bag made by Caroline Zoob; **66al** ph David Montgomery; **66ar,bl&br** ph Tom Leighton; **66cl&cr** ph Chris Everard; **67a&br** ph Christopher Drake/Enrica Stabile's houses in Le Thor, Provence & Brunello; **67bl** ph Debi Treloar/author, stylist and 'Caravan' (shop) owner Emily Chalmers and director Chris Richmond's home in London; **68** ph Debi Treloar/Debi Treloar's home in London; **69l** ph Debi Treloar/owner of Crème de la Crème à la Edgar, Helle Høgsbro Krag's home in Copenhagen; **69c** ph Sandra Lane; **69r** ph Catherine Gratwicke/the home of Patty Collister in London, owner of An Angel At My Table- painting from An Angel At My Table; **70** both ph Debi Treloar/owner of Crème de la Crème à la Edgar, Helle Høgsbro Krag's home in Copenhagen; **71al** ph Christopher Drake/Marisa Cavalli's home in Milan; **71ar** ph Debi Treloar/Ben Johns & Deb Waterman Johns' house in Georgetown; **71br** ph Debi Treloar/Victoria Andreae's house in London; **72al** ph Debi Treloar/designer Petra Boase & family's home in Norfolk; **72ar** ph Sandra Lane/Sophie Eadie's family home in London-strawberry cushions from The Cross; **72br** ph Sandra Lane/the home of Patty Collister in London, owner of An Angel At My Table–bed and quilt from An Angel At My Table, pillowcase made by Lucinda Ganderton; **73 main** ph Sandra Lane/Sophie Eadie's family home in London; **73l** inset ph Caroline Arber/patchwork blanket by Olga Tyrwhitt; **73r** inset ph Debi Treloar/designer Petra Boase & family's home in Norfolk; **74–75** ph Catherine Gratwicke, il Lizzie Sanders/café curtain made from children's hankies by Lucinda Ganderton; **76al** ph Debi Treloar/Victoria Andreae's

house in London; **76ar** ph Debi Treloar/owner of Crème de la Crème à la Edgar, Helle Høgsbro Krag's home in Copenhagen; **76cl** ph Debi Treloar/Ben Johns & Deb Waterman Johns' house in Georgetown; **76cr** ph Debi Treloar; **76bl** ph Catherine Gratwicke/cushion made by Greta Zoob; **76br** ph Catherine Gratwicke; **77** ph Debi Treloar/Cristine Tholstrup Hermansen and Helge Drenck's house in Copenhagen; **78–79** ph David Montgomery, il Michael Hill; **80** ph Caroline Arber/designed by Jane Cassini and Ann Brownfield; **81l** ph Sandra Lane; **81c** ph Catherine Gratwicke/studio of Sasha Gibb, colourist, interior consultant and designer-covered chair, handwork and printed length by Sasha Gibb; **81r** ph Debi Treloar/Mark and Sally of Baileys Home and Garden's house in Herefordshire; **82a** ph Debi Treloar/owner of Crème de la Crème à la Edgar, Helle Høgsbro Krag's home in Copenhagen; **82b** ph Polly Wreford; **83a** ph Debi Treloar/Cristine Tholstrup Hermansen and Helge Drenck's house in Copenhagen; **83b** ph Debi Treloar/the guesthouse of the interior designer & artist Philippe Guilmin, Brussels; **84a** Adamczewski, Hélène Adamczewski's shop in Lewes-apron made by Lattika Jain; **84b** ph Catherine Gratwicke/the home of Patty Collister in London, owner of An Angel At My Table; **85al** ph Catherine Gratwicke; **85ac&ar** ph Caroline Arber/designed and made by Jane Cassini and Ann Brownfield; **85bl** ph Polly Wreford; **85bc&br** ph Catherine Gratwicke; **86al,ac&cl** ph Polly Wreford; **86bl** ph Sandra Lane; **86ar** ph Caroline Arber/designed and made by Jane Cassini and Ann Brownfield; **86br** ph Debi Treloar/ Mark and Sally of Baileys Home and Garden's house in Herefordshire; **87** ph Caroline Arber/designed and made by Jane Cassini and Ann Brownfield; **88–89** ph David Montgomery, il Michael Hill; **90** ph Christopher Drake/Enrica Stabile's house, Le Thor, Provence; tablecloth, cushions & teacup, L'Utile e il Dilettevole; **91l** ph Christopher Drake/ iron bed, antique bedspread & cushions from L'Utile e il Dilettevole; **91c** ph Francesca Yorke; **91r** ph Catherine Gratwicke; **92al** ph Christopher Drake/Mr & Mrs Degrugillier, Le Mas de Flore, Antiquite et Creation, Lagnes, Isle sur Sorgue, Provence-garden table & chair from Le Mas de Flore, cushion from l'Utile e il Dilettevole; **92ar&b** ph Christopher Drake/designer Barbara Davis' own house in upstate New York; **93a** ph Christopher Drake/Enrica Stabile's house in Brunello; **93b** ph Christopher Drake/Guido & Marilea Somaré's house in Milan-garden chair, l'Utile e il Dilettevole; **94** ph Christopher Drake/La Bastide Rose, Nicole & Pierre Salinger's house, Le Thor, Provence- iron bed, garden chair, tin candlestick, cotton bag, antique bedspread & all cushions, L'Utile e il Dilettevole; **95al** ph Christopher Drake/Enrica Stabile's house in Provence; cushion & throw, L'Utile e il Dilettevole; **95ac** ph Sandra Lane/cushions and throw from Une Histoire Simple; **95ar** ph Catherine Gratwicke/peg bag made by Lattika Jain; **95b** Sandra Lane/cushions and throw from Cath Kidston; **96al,bl,cr&ar** all ph Francesca Yorke; **96cl** ph Marianne Majerus; **96br** ph Francesca Yorke/artist Marylin Phipps' house in Kent; **97a** ph Caroline Arber/designed and made by Jane Cassini and Ann Brownfield; **97bl&br** ph Christopher Drake; **98–99** ph Marianne Majerus, il Michael Hill/wire-work basket designer Jane Seabrook at The Chelsea Gardener.

business credits

ADAMCZEWSKI
88 High Street
Lewes
East Sussex BN7 1XN
t. 01273 470105
adamczewski@onetel.net.uk
Fine houseware.
Page **84a**

AN ANGEL AT MY TABLE
116A Fortess Road
Tufnell Park
London NW5 2HL
t. 020 7424 9777
f. 020 7424 9666
www.angelatmytable.co.uk
Painted furniture and accessories.
Pages **3, 4, 17al, 18a, 44b, 62inset, 69r, 72b, 84b**

ANNA MASSEE OF HET GROTE AVONTUUR
Het Grote Avontuur
Haarlemmerstraat 25
1013 EJ Amsterdam
t. 020 6268597
www.hetgroteavontuur.nl
Pages **14, 30b, 55bl**

ANNELIE BRUIJN
t. +31 653 702869
annelie_bruijn@email.com
Page **30ar**

ANTHROPOLOGIE
t. +800 309 2500
www.anthropologie.com
Page **49ar**

BAILEYS HOME & GARDEN
The Engine Shed
Station Approach
Ross-on-Wye
Herefordshire HR9 7BW
t. 01989 563015
f. 01989 768172
www.baileyshomeandgarden.com
Pages **12al, 12ar, 45a, 81r, 86br**

BARBARA DAVIS
Designer
t. +1 607 264 3673
Pages **92al, 92b**

BENNISON
16 Holbein Place
London SW1W 8NL
t. 020 7730 8076
bennisonfabrics@btinternet.com
www.bennisonfabrics.com
Page **42**

BOIS-RENARD
t. +1 215 247 4777
Decorative home accessories.
Pages **19ar, 63ar**

CARLA SAIBENE
Carla Saibene (shop)
via San Maurilio 20
Milano
Italy
t/f. +39 2 77 33 15 70
xaibsrl@yahoo.com
Womenswear collection, accessories and antiques.
Page **49al**

CAROLINE ZOOB
Shop A
33 Cliffe High Street
Lewes
East Sussex BN7 2AN
t. 01273 476464 (shop & mail order)
www.carolinezoob.com
Hand-made collectables.
Pages **8c, 64–65**

CECILIE TELLE
cecilietelle@hotmail.com
t. 020 7272 1335
Felted wool products for children & adults, and for the kitchen.
Page **36al**

CLAUDIA BRYANT
t. 020 7602 2852
Pages **28, 34, 63al**

CRÈME DE LA CRÈME À LA EDGAR
Kompagnistræde 8,st
1208 Copenhagen K
t. +45 33361818
Pages **69l, 70 both, 76ar, 82a**

CUNNINGHAM FURNITURE
t. 020 8674 1743
Page **30al**

DEBI TRELOAR
www.debitreloar.com
Pages **19ac, 19bc, 68**

EMMA GREENHILL
egreenhill@freenet.co.uk
Pages **1, 11c, 15b**

EMILY CHALMERS
Author & stylist
emily@emilychalmers.com
Caravan (shop)
11 Lamb Street
Spitalfields
London E1 6EA
t. 020 7247 6467
www.caravanstyle.com
Pages **6c, 67bl**

EMILY MEDLEY
Designer
emilymedley@mac.com
Pages **28, 34–35, 51br**

ENRICA STABILE
L'Utile e il Dilettevole (shop)
Via Carlo Maria Maggi 6
20154 Milano
t. +39 0234 53 60 86
www.enricastabile.com
Antiques dealer, interior decorator and photographic stylist.
Pages **32al, 67a, 67br, 90, 91l, 93, 94, 95al**

FRANCESCA MILLS
Designer/stylist
t. 020 7733 9193
f. 020 7274 8861
Page **16a**

**HOGGY'S ANTIQUES TOYS &
TEXTILES AT SHARLAND & LEWIS**
52 Long Street
Tetbury
Gloucester GL8 8AQ
t. 01666 500354
www.sharlandandlewis.com
Page **61 inset**

THE HOUSEMADE
Sue West
t/f. 01453 757771
sue.west@btopenworld.com
Interior & product design
Page **55br**

JANE CASSINI
jane_vintagestyle@yahoo.com
Pages **7l,11l, 19br, 26ar, 33al, 33ac, 39bl,
51a, 54bl, 80, 85ac, 85ar, 86ar, 87, 97a**

KAREN NICOL EMBROIDERY
t. 020 8979 4593
Pages **17ar, 18bl, 20–21, 25ar,
48al, 56–57**

LATTIKA JAIN
t. 020 8682 3088
*Freelance in textile design, fashion &
knitwear.*
Pages **33ar, 84a, 95ar**

LUCY SALEM
t. 020 8563 2625
lucyandmarcsalem@hotmail.com
*Makes and sources soft furnishings
and decorative items for the home*
Pages **16b, 18br, 44b, 55a, 63al, 63br**

LULU GUINNESS
3 Ellis Street
London SW1X 9AL
t. 020 7823 4828
f. 020 7823 4889
www.luluguinness.com
Pages **15ar, 17b, 26ac, 27 main, 39a, 58**

MAISONETTE
t. 020 8964 8444
f. 08964 8464
maisonette.uk@aol.com
www.maisonette.uk.com
Pages **2, 16a, 38b**

MARISA CAVALLI
via Solferino, 11
20121 Milano
Italy
t. +39 02 36 51 14 49
f. +39 02 29 00 18 60
marisacavalli@hotmail.com
Page **71al**

OLGA TYRWHITT
tyrwhitt@ntlworld.com
Textile artist, courses available
Pages **73 inset left**

PETRA BOASE
www.petraboase.com
info@petraboase.com
Pages **17ac, 27 inset, 43l, 45b, 60al,
72al, 73 inset right**

PHILIPPE GUILMIN
Interior designer & artist
philippe.guilmin@skynet.be
Pages **6l, 29r, 60b, 83b**

RÜTZOU A/S
t. +45 35 24 06 16
f. +45 35 24 06 15
www.rutzou.com
cph@rutzou.com
Pages **18–19, 37, 55cl**

SASHA GIBB
t/f. 01534 863211
home@sashagibb.co.uk
*Interior and colour consultant
Contemporary home furnishings designed
and made from vintage blankets*
Pages **36al, 81c**

STUDIO AANDACHT
ben.lambers@studioaandacht.nl
www.studioaandacht.nl
Art direction and interior production.
Page **15al**

SUSANNAH
25 Broad Street
Bath
BA1 5LW
Pages **50bl, 50bc**

THE CHELSEA GARDENER
125 Sydney Street
Kings Road
London SW3 6NR
t. 020 7352 5656
f. 020 7352 3301
www.chelseagardener.com
Pages **98–99**

acknowledgments

Although it is my name that appears on the title page, this book is very much a joint project with the editorial, creative and production teams at RP&S. I would like to thank everybody who has made it possible and especially Miriam for her editorial guidance, Anne-Marie for her art direction, Emily for once again selecting such interesting pictures, and Megan for putting them all together on the page.

Copyright information
(continued from page 4)
All projects have been previously published by Ryland, Peters & Small

Page 20 Ethereal Throw by Karen Nicol. Previously published in *Cushions, Pillows & Throws* by Lucinda Ganderton, © 2003.

Page 22 Transfer Print Cushion by Lucinda Ganderton. Previously published in *Cushions, Pillows & Throws* by Lucinda Ganderton, © 2003.

Page 34 Apron by Emily Medley. Previously published in *Vintage Fabric Style* by Lucinda Ganderton and Rose Hammick, © 2003.

Page 40 Heart of Fresh Roses by Paula Pryke. Previously published in *Wreaths & Garlands* by Paula Pryke, © 1998.

Page 46 Voile Bed Canopy by Katrin Cargill. Previously published in *Simple Beds* by Katrin Cargill, © 1998.

Page 52 Diamond Bedcover by Jeanie Blake. Previously published in *Cushions, Pillows & Throws* by Lucinda Ganderton, © 2003.

Page 56 Diamanté Cushion by Karen Nicol. Previously published in *Cushions, Pillows & Throws* by Lucinda Ganderton, © 2003.

Page 64 Floral Dorothy Bag by Caroline Zoob. Previously published in *Cushions, Pillows & Throws* by Lucinda Ganderton, © 2003.

Page 74 Handkerchief Curtain by Lucinda Ganderton. Previously published in *Vintage Fabric Style* by © Lucinda Ganderton and Rose Hammick, © 2003.

Page 78 Pull-along Duck by Stewart & Sally Walton. Previously published in *Painted Woodcraft* by Sally and Stewart Walton, © 1997.

Page 88 Letter Rack by Stewart & Sally Walton. Previously published in *Painted Woodcraft* by Sally and Stewart Walton, © 1997.

Page 98 Wirework Basket by Jane Seabrook. Previously published in *Containers* by George Carter, © 1997.